The Amazing Mary Higgs

C M Talbot

OWC Publishing

First Published in 2011 by

Oldham Writing Café - OWC Publishing

ISBN   978-0-9565410-1-7

© C M Talbot 2011

A CIP record for this book is available from the British Library.

Printed and bound by
Think Ink
Fountain Way,
Reydon Business Park,
Reydon,
Suffolk,
IP18 6DH

(3rd print run) 2013

Cover design by Gemma Hall

Dedication

To my wonderful family for their help,
support and encouragement.

Contents

Acknowledgements

I am very grateful for all the help given to me by family, friends and staff at various libraries and archives.

For reading, editing and advising: Craig Talbot, Gabrielle Carlin, Mary Pendlebury, Elizabeth Bailey, Paul Price and members of Oldham Writing Café.

For her research idea and help: Maureen (Moie) Burns of Oldham and later Tameside Local Studies Libraries.

For help and support with records, photographs and archives and for permission to use photographs: the staff at the Oldham Chronicle, Oldham Local Studies Library and Archives, especially Roger Ivens and Sue Smith, Oldham Museum, particularly Sean Baggaley, Bradford Local Studies Library, Bradford Girls' Grammar School, Manchester Girl's Grammar School, Greenwich Local Studies, Girton College Archives and Rev. Neil Chappell of Greenacres Congregational Church.

For oral and written information: Mary's grandchildren in the USA, the late Edith Hall and Barbara Bergman and great grandchildren, Sheila Hall and Jay Bergman.

For help and advice with printing and publishing: Lois Mellor, Freda Millett and Carolyn Crossley.

For cover design: Gemma Hall.

My husband Nigel has kept me going and has always been around to chauffer me to many places, to take photos and give help, advice and encouragement.

The amount of support has been marvellous, particularly as this project has taken rather a long time to complete.

Any final mistakes are mine. If I have left anyone out, please accept my thanks and apologies. Cheers everyone!

Preface

Over 120 years ago, Reverend Higgs brought with his wife Mary and their four children to live in Oldham. This was an era when women were not expected to become involved in issues outside the home. However, Mary had been a student, college lecturer and teacher before her career had been cut short by marriage. She began to devote what time she could to social and environmental issues in the town. One of her early initiatives was to set up of a 'rescue home' for homeless women.

I first heard of Mary Higgs when I was looking for a research topic for a dissertation. A member of staff at Oldham Local Studies Library, Maureen Burns, suggested that Mary would make an interesting subject. When I started to read books, articles and letters written by Mary, I was surprised that the name of this remarkable woman was not more widely known in the town. I was particularly fascinated by the fact that she dressed as a tramp and stayed in workhouses and common lodging houses in the early 20th century. This was 30 years before George Orwell's experiences being *Down and Out in Paris and London.*

Early in 2007, Jupiter TV asked me for information about Mary's life when they were producing a BBC4 series *The Edwardians.* One programme, entitled *Winners and Losers* featured Mary Higgs and other Edwardians. It was presented by Dan Snow and shown on 16th May and repeated in June.

Mary was accompanied on her undercover investigations by an anonymous friend. During my extensive research, I discovered the woman's identity. I felt that it was appropriate to tell the story of Mary Higgs through the eyes of her companion, Annie Lee, a cotton worker who later became the superintendant of a hostel for homeless women.

The early life of Mary, before she came to Oldham, is told from Mary's view point.

All the main characters are real and the important facts are true. The names of minor characters, some scenes, and dialogue are the work of fiction. Annie died in 1927, ten years earlier than Mary; therefore, there is some artistic licence with regard to their relationship in those later years.

Mary Ann Higgs (nee Kingsland) aged about 18

Introduction

My name is Annie Lee and I was born in 1860 in Wolverhampton. I spent most of my life in the northern town of Oldham and that is where I got to know an amazing woman who had a great influence on my life.

Looking back, I remember the summer 1903. It was almost 8 pm by the time Mary and I, weary and soaked through to the skin, reached the workhouse in West Yorkshire. We had not eaten anything for seven hours and started our journey at 2 pm but had misjudged the distance and had difficulty finding the place; partly due to the misleading directions we had been given. Having walked over 11 miles, we had begun to worry that we might be too late to be admitted for the night. The rain had seeped through the holes in our boots and our well-worn skirts and shawls were sodden. The battered umbrella we had shared had given little protection against the downpour. With low spirits we entered the large stone lodge to find a lone man in the office. We were relieved to see that he looked respectable but our confidence was short lived, for after he had taken our details, he began to suggest that Mary, as a married woman needed to 'sleep warm' and made it clear that he was offering himself for the job.

I knew little of Mary's life before she came to Oldham. Therefore, the following is Mary's account of the early experiences that shaped her ideas.

PART 1 – MARY

Chapter 1 Mary's Early Life

I have happy memories of my early childhood spent in Rowde, near the lovely market town of Devizes in Wiltshire. I was born Mary Ann Kingsland in the February of 1854 to Caroline and William Kingsland. Mother, eight years older than father and the daughter of a timber merchant and Borough Magistrate in Truro Cornwall, had been brought up in a household with three live-in servants. Becoming the wife of a modestly paid Congregational minister had meant a large drop in living standards for mother, but we did have a servant who lived with us to help in the house. This was just as well because by 1857 she had given birth to my two brothers, William and John. My father, William, was from Kent but trained for the ministry in Devon.

Rowde was a well-wooded area with a number of thatched cottages. We enjoyed the green and pleasant environment and the mild climate of the southwest. This was to change in 1862 when my father was offered a post at College Chapel in Bradford, West Yorkshire. At that time, Bradford was a bustling, smoky, industrial town. The cold, damp climate and the poor living and working conditions of most of the inhabitants were a shock to the system of my rather delicate mother.

My brothers and I were initially educated at home. When I reached 13, I went to a school run by a lady named Miss Stott. This was, I believe, the best girls' school in Bradford and I later realised how fortunate I was to enjoy this education when most girls of my age in the industrial north were working.

My father was eager for me to be involved in church activities. By the age of 13, I was a Sunday school teacher and a member of the church choir. These activities brought me into contact with the poorer members of the area. I visited the homes of my pupils and became aware of how different some of the lifestyles were from my own. The choir sang in many venues including common lodging houses, places regularly used by prostitutes. I could not have foreseen that many years later I would stay in places like that myself.

One day I overheard my father lamenting, 'If Mary had been a boy, something could have been made of her.'

Questioning one's parents was not acceptable but privately I asked myself why something could not equally be made of a girl. After all, I had been educated with my brothers at home and could see no difference between the minds of boys and girls. Spurred on by this and determined to prove my worth, I continued to work hard at my studies. I passed the junior and senior Cambridge examinations and gained a scholarship, which was financed by the local authority of Leeds and supplemented by Bradford.

In late August 1871, all the family went with me to Bradford station to wish me well. My trunk had been sent ahead so I did not have a great deal to carry on the journey. After a tearful goodbye, I settled into my compartment. I tried to read but I was too excited and a little worried about all the connections. I had to change at Leeds and then again at Peterborough. The time passed quicker than I thought it would, mainly because I was interested in looking out of the window at places I had not seen before. It did not seem long before the train pulled in at Hitchin station. Collecting my belongings, I stepped out onto the platform.

'Miss Kingsland?'

I turned to see a man about 30 looking at me.

'Yes, that's me. Hello,' I said holding out my hand.

He looked unsure about whether it would be appropriate to take it, so I quickly put it back to my side and gave him my bag instead.

'This way, Miss.'

'And you are?'

'I'm Burrows Miss, the gardener.'

He walked purposefully with me trotting behind. I was becoming quite breathless but whether it was the exertion or my excitement, I wasn't sure. He helped me into the buggy and without another word, urged his horse on its way.

I like to talk so I asked,

'Is it far?'

'No, not far,'

I longed to ask questions.

'What's it like?'

'What?'

'Benslow House. What's it like? What are the students like?'

'You'll have to see for yourself, Miss.'

I was eager to get to the place that would be my new home. The College for Women - the first in Britain - had opened two year earlier in 1869 with just five students. I was to be part of a small group of 12 students. How very exciting for an 18-year-old, who had rarely left Bradford. There was a lot of fluttering in my insides as I approached the door of the large brick building. I assumed it had been built as the residence of a well-to-do family. Now it was to be the home of this rather shy, but excitable young woman.

Benslow House in Hitchen, Hertfordshire

I was shown into the library where some students were talking while others read. Most of them appeared mature and self assured. One or two, I noticed, wore rather expensive dresses. It felt as though I had stood for a long time looking round, when a girl got up and greeted me warmly.

'Welcome. You must be Miss Kingsland. I'm Rachel, Rachel Cook. Pleased to meet you.' She held out her hand.

'Please call me Mary. Oh Rachel I'm so pleased to meet you too.'

'How was your journey?' asked Rachel.

'It was fine. The time went so quickly.'

'What a pretty costume.'

'Thank you, mother made it.'

'Dark blue suits you.'

'Miss Kingsland?' enquired a young woman, whom I presumed from her dress and manner was a servant.

'Yes,' I replied.

'Miss Davies would like to see you now. I'm to take you to her room.' I smiled at Rachel as I got up, straightened my velvet skirt, and followed the young woman along the hall and up an impressive staircase. All the doors were panelled wood. The servant stopped at one and knocked gently. A quiet voice told us to 'come in.'

The woman sitting behind the desk got to her feet. My first impression of Miss Davies was one of surprise and I think a little

disappointment. I had expected to meet someone with a commanding presence. I knew Miss Davies was a campaigner for women's suffrage and higher education. She had fought hard and written *The Higher Education of Women* as part of her campaign to persuade others to help her in this venture. It must have taken an incredible amount of perseverance and strength of character to achieve it. The woman, who greeted me cordially but gently, was rather mouse-like. She addressed me quietly as her small eyes, which looked out from a very ordinary face, met mine. Just a little of her light brown hair had dared to escape from the front of her white cap. Her high-necked dress was dark and severe. Her movements were small and restrained and to my young eyes, it was a very reserved look. However, I was to find out that it is wrong to judge a woman by her appearance. After our short interview, I was shown around the house. The dining room was in the basement. There were two tables, one for the students, and one for the mistress (head) and her friends. I was told that Miss Davies did not live at the college, but that on her visits, she sat with the mistress at her table. Some of the rooms, such as the library were used for a number of different activities. Meetings were held there and the Choral Society practiced in the room. I vowed I would make the most of every moment of my time there and that is just what I did. Some groups had already been formed and others were starting. I joined the Choral Society, the Shakespeare Reading Group and the Acting Group. If I had any spare time, I enjoyed dancing and writing humorous verse.

When the college opened in 1869 the first students were; Rachel Cook, Emily Gibson, Louisa Lumsden, Adelaide Manning, Sarah Woodhead and Isabella Townshend. Miss Davies had formulated a scheme of work which was the same as that for male students at Cambridge. She had been very frustrated that her brother had enjoyed a college education while she, a girl, had been denied it. Therefore she was adamant that our education would be in no way inferior. By 1871, the student numbers were in double figures. There was only room in the house to accommodate eight students, so I slept with three others in the lodge. One young woman even had to sleep in the gardener's cottage. None of this was a hardship; we knew we were privileged pioneers but our location made things rather difficult. Male lecturers had to travel nearly 30 miles from Cambridge by train. However, a small number of female lecturers lived in the house.

Although I enjoyed writing, science was my passion. I was the first woman to study natural science to the same level as men. It was particularly difficult for me without access to a laboratory, but the lecturer who came from Cambridge brought specimens for me to observe through a microscope. I worked hard at my studies and learned a great deal from those around me. Not surprisingly, many of our discussions were about women's equality. We knew how fortunate we were, but felt that this opportunity should be much more widely available. Miss Davies had been an enthusiastic campaigner for women's suffrage before she embarked on her ambitious scheme to set up a college for young women. As students we were able to discuss these matters and were greatly influenced by each other. Can you imagine the excitement when our first three students took and passed what were known as the Tripos Examinations? Rachel Cook and Louisa Lumsden, who passed in classical studies and Sarah Woodhead, who passed in mathematics, were indeed pioneers in women's education.

When the students found they had passed, flags were hoisted, bells were rung and songs were sung. Rachel climbed on to the college roof to sing, '*Gaudeamus Igitur*'

Mary is on the left at the back

an old student song written in Latin and dating from the 13th century, including the words,

'Long live our academy, Teachers whom we cherish: Long live all the graduates; And the undergraduates, Ever may they flourish.'
How we all cheered! I knew they were making history and I was so proud to be a part of it.

1st 2nd 3rd year students 1871-1872

Left to right
Back row - R. Cook, E. Welsh, L. Lumsden,
S.Woodhead, A. Bulley, M. Hoskins
Mid row - M. Kingsland, R. Aitken, J. Dove
Front row - E. Gibson, I. Townshend, I.Gamble

Benslow House had been acquired on lease and it was soon seen that it would be necessary to find a larger permanent building. With the financial backing of Barbara Bodichon and other supporters, land at Girton was purchased in 1871. Miss Davies and Mrs. Bodichon (nee Leigh Smith) were members of the London Suffrage Committee, founded in 1866. Another member was Elizabeth Garrett (later Garrett Anderson), who became Britain's first female doctor and first mayor.

Mrs. Bodichon, the illegitimate daughter of the radical MP Benjamin Leigh-Smith, was given an allowance by her father. This enabled her to support the plans of Miss Davies.

Work started on what would be the first women's college at Cambridge. Girton was about two miles outside Cambridge, probably because it wasn't considered a good idea for us to be too near the male students! Alfred Waterhouse, the architect of the Natural History Museum in London and Manchester Town Hall, designed Girton College.The stately, red brick establishment was to house a tutor and 15 students.

In 1873, we were on the move. At last, I was near enough to attend lectures at Trinity College Cambridge. I was privileged to have the support of Michael Foster, Professor of Physiology at the College. He was responsible for introducing new methods of studying biology and physiology that emphasized laboratory training and practical follow-up work by the students. Unfortunately women were not allowed to sit with the male students, so I had to sit in the gallery and take notes. Nevertheless, room was made for a microscope and Professor Foster and his assistants ran up and down the steps, bringing specimens to look at and giving guidance. I continued to work hard and enjoyed a wide social life. I joined the Christian Student Movement and enjoyed dancing, plays and musical performances. I found an outlet for my sense of fun and wrote humorous parodies such as *The Groan of the Plucked Goose*. I even started a college joke book and wrote what I hoped would be a rousing farewell song. I put the words to the tune of the Canadian Boat song. Here's a snatch;

First and last chorus
Go sisters go – the world is wide
And dangers many may you betide
But nought from you our love shall hide.
Last verse
Smoothly on ocean's tide ye launch
Your headsail clear and your hearts are staunch
Take with you love of Girton's name
And raise her great and worthy fame.

Miss Davies was keen to extend the teaching staff by retaining 'old students'. Louisa Lumsden was by then a tutor in classics. In November 1874, while I was studying for my December examination, it was suggested that I stay on at the college in a teaching capacity. I knew that another final year student, Jane Dove, would also like to be retained so I felt that she should be told about the proposal. Jane, in turn, told Louisa who voiced her concerns to Miss Davies. Louisa's objection was that I was too young and socially inferior. She obviously considered this scholarship funded, Congregational minister's daughter, to have too low a status to be a lecturer. Louisa's background was very different from mine. When she entered the college at the age of 28, she had already attended a progressive boarding school near Brussels, followed by two years at a finishing school in London. She had also attended lectures in her home city of Edinburgh. In fact, she had received a much better education than the founder of the college, Miss Davies. Louisa felt that if retained, I should sit with the students. She felt this so strongly that she even threatened to resign. Miss Davies wrote to Mrs. Barbara Bodichon, a supporter of the College and member of the governing committee. It is clear from the letter that Miss Davies disapproved of the way Louisa had behaved in the matter. She went as far as to say that she did not think Louisa would ever make a suitable mistress. Thankfully, it is also obvious from her correspondence that Miss Davies disagreed with the view that I was childish.

4th November 1874

Dear Mrs. Bodichon,

I have talked to Miss Kingsland about the possibility of her coming back to us next term and taking part in the teaching. She wishes it much, but referred the decision to her parents who are considering it. I asked of course merely whether in case the offer should be made by the committee, she could accept it. Her instinct of loyalty induced her to tell Miss Dove, as she knew she wished for it herself, and she told Miss Lumsden, who therefore came to me to ask if Miss K's (Kingsland's) position would be the same as hers, as if so, she must resign. I told her that Miss K being so much younger, her position would of course be different, but I was not prepared with exact definitions. Accordingly, she suggested that she should not sit at our table and should otherwise remain in the position of student. I think this unreasonable, and I am not at all afraid of Miss L's resigning. She seems quite bent upon staying. I am afraid we must give up our hope of her ever being fit to be Mistress. She has come out very badly in this business, having been so indiscreet as to discuss it, not only with two or three of the older students but with Miss Kilgour! On the other hand, Miss K's (Kingsland's) way of receiving the ideas made me wish for her still more than before. Miss L's objections to her are her social inferiority and the ignorance of conventional manners that it entails, and her alleged childishness (which I do not see). There is a proposal of a position for Miss Dove at Cheltenham, with Miss Beale.

My parents were happy to support my stay at the College. Miss Davies wrote again to Mrs. Bodichon about the matter on 10th November. She was critical about the way in which the matter was being openly discussed before it had been put before the committee. Louisa was obviously confident enough to disagree forcibly with the views of Miss Davies. She was the youngest member of the staff and many of the students wanted her to speak on their behalf in committee meetings. Miss Davies strongly disapproved of this.

The meeting of the Executive Committee took place on Monday 30th November at 5 pm, and the proposal to retain me as a teacher of mathematics was discussed. Despite some opposition, Miss Davies got her way and the decision to allow me to stay was taken. Although the women at the college were advantaged compared to other women of the day, we did not have the facilities available to the male students. This was a particular problem for the study of science. Despite all these constraints, I overcame the difficulties and became the very first woman to take the Natural Science Tripos, gaining second-class honours in 1874. Women's higher education was in its infancy and we had played our part in pushing forward the boundaries in the fight for female equality in education. But even though our studies were at the same level as those of the male students, the conventions of the time meant that we were not awarded degrees.

After passing the Tripos examinations, I began lecturing in mathematics and science. Miss Davies appreciated my lectures and teaching skills but by the following April I had decided to leave the College. Miss Davies wrote to Mrs. Bodichon on 22nd April 1875.

Miss Kingsland is giving lectures on physiology with a microscope and blackboard. Her teaching will be a great loss as to Natural Science, as we know no students nearly ready to take that up. But I cannot attempt to persuade her to stay on and miss the chance of the appointment at Bradford.

I had been offered a position of teacher of science and mathematics at the newly built Grammar School for Girls in Bradford. However, I could not take up the position until the end of September and Miss Davies was keen for me to stay on at Girton until then. She had already discussed it with the mistress, Marianne Bernard, when she wrote to Barbara Bodichon.

I have talked to Miss Bernard about Miss Kingsland, as she quite wishes to have her back, I shall nominate her at the next meeting.

Another committee member, Fanny Metcalfe disagreed with Miss Davies' decision to keep me on when she knew that I would be leaving soon, believing that it was not conducive to good teaching. She was not happy about the fact that she had not been consulted. Miss Davies did not always agree with the other members of the committee. This sometimes resulted in accusations of her being autocratic. Miss Metcalfe criticized Miss Davies' behaviour in a letter to Miss Bodichon. However, Miss Davies got her way and I stayed at the college, lecturing in mathematics and science for 18 months, until the school in Bradford was ready for me. One of my students, who became the next lecturer in science, was Constance Herschel, youngest daughter of the astronomer, Sir John Herschel.

As students, we had been able to debate issues of the day with other like-minded women and being such a small group had a great influence on each other. A celebratory song was written about those first pioneers. It was sung enthusiastically and raucously and not in an entirely ladylike manner, by the students to the tune of the *'British Grenadiers'*.

> *And when the goal is won, girls,*
> *And women get degrees,*
> *We'll cry, 'Long live the three girls,*

Who showed the way to these!
Who showed the way we follow,
Who knew no doubts or fears,
Our Woodhead, Cook and Lumsden,
The Girton Pioneers!'

Louisa Lumsden finally decided that she could no longer work with Miss Davies and resigned in 1875. She took up an appointment as classics tutor at Cheltenham College and persuaded another student, Constance Maynard to join her. Two years later, they were involved in the founding of St. Leonard's Girls' School in St. Andrews, Fife. Louise, aged 37, became its first headmistress and Constance took up another senior position. Jane Dove joined them as science tutor. Louisa believed that *'a girl should receive an education as good as her brother's, if not better'* and was a lover of physical pursuits including the unladylike sport of wrestling. She is credited with introducing lacrosse into the school curriculum after her visit to North America. Constance and Louisa had a close but often stormy relationship for a number of years. Eventually Constance went her own way, and with the financial backing of Ann Dudin Brown, founded Westfield College, Hampstead, London, becoming its first headmistress in 1882. I remained friends with Miss Davies and Constance Maynard for many years.

It is not surprising that the two other pioneers Sarah Woodhead and Rachel Cook shared life-long interests in the education of girls and went on to have high profile roles in girls' education At Girton we threw ourselves ardently into the plea for women's education and suffrage causes which I continued to support for the rest of my life. However, although I began on the same path as most of those young women, teaching at a school for girls, my life was later to take a very different route.

Girton College: Outside and Inside Views

Chapter 2 Teaching and Marriage

At the age of 21 I left behind the college life I had enjoyed so much and moved back north. As I entered a new phase of my life, I found myself once more at the forefront of girls' education, but in a different arena. The Endowed Schools Act of 1869 had paved the way for an enthusiastic group in Bradford to set about raising funds to establish a school for girls. The forward-thinking patrons believed that it was desirable to provide scholarships for the daughters of working men. They also promised funds to enable girls from poorer families to go to the newly emerging colleges such as Girton and Newnham, Cambridge. Nonetheless, with fees of four guineas (four pounds and four shillings) per term or 12 guineas per annum, most of the students at the school were the daughters of professional or merchant families.

Bradford Girls' Grammar School, Hallfield Road, opened its doors on Monday 27th September 1875. At the official opening, speeches were given on the subject of education for girls. Patron and MP William Edward Forster said that he supported the idea of a day school for girls rather than a boarding school. Another MP, Sir Matthew Wilson, also spoke in favour of education for girls, criticising the prevailing attitude of the time. The view that girls should not be encouraged to think and learn was, he said, reflected in the often-used rhyme,

> *'Be to their faults a little blind,*
> *But put a padlock on their mind.'*

One of the speakers claimed that this was the first high school in England offering education of the highest level to girls between the ages of seven and 19. It was also one of the first girls' schools to introduce physical education. This was a radical idea at a time when many thought that girls should not be encouraged in physical pursuits. When the school first opened there were 109 pupils, and by the end of the first year this had risen to 198. The first headmistress was Miss Mary E. Potter, the former headmistress of the Chelsea High School for Girls. Most of the staff had not had the advantage of a college education.

Bradford Girls' Grammar School

Therefore, despite my age, I was made to feel a valued member of the staff. This was a very special school offering French, German, science and physical education to the girls of Bradford. It is hardly surprising that I felt privileged to start my teaching career at such a groundbreaking establishment. I had 'coached' girls at Girton but privately believed that this had not equipped me to stand before a class. I was very nervous as I walked into the classroom on the first day.

Through my involvement with the church I met a handsome young theology student, Thomas Kilpin Higgs. After a short courtship we became engaged in 1876. Life was good. Our family was living comfortably with father in the ministry, I was happily teaching and my two younger brothers were working in the Bradford woollen trade. It had been intended, in addition to my teaching, that I should become a sort of curate for my father.

Miss Mary Potter

Then, quite suddenly, our world changed. Dear father became seriously ill. Despite spending some time in the south with my mother to get the benefit of cleaner air, he did not recover. He died of consumption in 1876 at the age of 49. What a shock to us all! At that time there was a slump in the woollen trade, so both my brothers changed occupation. William began training to be an engineer and John decided to prepare for the ministry. In a short time, my role had gone from privileged student and teacher to family breadwinner and support for my delicate mother for the next three years. This was to be first of many serious illnesses and premature deaths that were to affect my life. Yet my (generally) resilient nature and my trust in God helped me adapt to the situation. I enjoyed the challenge and personal satisfaction of teaching. I remember a girl who arrived in my class unable to do any sums correctly. I felt pride and a wonderful feeling of triumph for the girl and myself, when she passed the examination and moved on to the next level. There were eight classes; each teacher was in charge of a class, but also taught their specialist subjects to other classes. I taught botany to my own class and science to the higher classes. In 1878 I was very proud when six of our girls passed the Cambridge Local Examination with distinction in zoology, the subject I had taught. I was also very pleased to hear that two of my students who had gained scholarships to Girton College and Newnham Hall Cambridge were making good progress.

The general depression in the woollen trade caused the early and sudden removal of some pupils who would otherwise have remained longer. However, the parents of the area must have appreciated the value of our school, because in 1879 the number of pupils continued to rise despite the opening of a Higher Board School in the vicinity.

As one of the first female teachers of science, my knowledge and skills were in great demand. Therefore, I was asked by Titus Salt, a school governor, to teach at another school in the Bradford area one day a week. Titus Salt was an imposing portly man of around 70 with bushy eyebrows and a huge, thick white beard and I was rather in awe of him. The philanthropic woollen manufacturer was concerned about the health and moral welfare of his many employees. He decided to create a small town with decent quality houses, schools and a Congregational church for his workers. I noted that there was no public house in Saltaire.

It was at this time that I met another man who was to have a lasting effect on my developing ideas. William T. Stead, a governor of the school, was to be an inspiration in my quest for social reform in later years. The Salt Schools, as they were collectively known, had separate high schools for boys and girls. Unusually, the boys' school opened a year after the school for girls. The prospectus for the girls' school stated that,

'The Saltaire Girls' High School was established with the object of placing within the reach of the inhabitants of Shipley, Saltaire, and the surrounding districts, a high class day school, where, at a modest cost, sound and thorough education under well-trained teachers could be offered to Girls.'

Titus Salt

Although it was hoped that the fees would put the school within the reach of working families, most girls were from professional families with a small number of tradesmen's daughters. Here is an example of fathers' occupations as stated in the registers of 1877 to 1878; pawnbroker, share-broker, maltster, drapers' agent, merchant, corn manufacturer, accountant, straw hat manufacturer, gentleman, woollen draper, plumber, inn keeper and spinner.

Miss Medina Sarah Griffiths, a former teacher of mine, was headmistress of the girls' school. The school provided a wide curriculum, including languages and art. I taught science and mathematics to the older girls. Miss Griffiths had very strong ideas about the education of girls. In her address at what was called the first 'school entertainment' she asked,

'For what am I training these children? For life as the beginning of eternity. It is a mistake to think that children come to school to acquire a certain amount of knowledge, a stock of furniture for their life-house. Not so is it, but rather to learn to use the tools by which they may make the furniture. What is the ideal I hold before me? A true woman as strong in body as judicious care and exercise can make her, as fearless and brave in heart as a God-fearing life and a happy creed can form her; faithful in all domestic duties; true in all womanly relationships, one who can enjoy and engage in rational conversation; who is quick to see need, ready to help, and as earnest and skilful in the commonplace duties of home life as in intellectual pursuits; a women who makes life nobler by her influence, who can think, act, and speak intelligently.'

She also had very firm views when it came to rewards and punishments. There were no marks given except for final examinations and no prizes, therefore no prize-giving ceremonies and no punishments. There is no doubt that I was influenced by Miss Griffiths for whom I had the greatest respect and who remained a life-long friend. What did I gain from this experience and to what extent was I to fulfil Miss Griffith's ideal? Time would tell. There was another change on the horizon. In August 1879 at the age of 25, I married 28-year-old Reverend Thomas Kilpin Higgs at College Chapel, Bradford, where my father had been the minister. As I stood at the altar, surrounded my family, friends and well-wishing members of the congregation, I could never have guessed that 20 years later, I would return to that area, but instead of a bridal gown, I would be wearing the clothes of a tramp.

My husband, Thomas Higgs, was born in Ipswich, Suffolk. He qualified as an engineer before gaining a Master of Arts at the Victoria University of Manchester. He then went on to study Theology at Lancashire Independent College, Whalley Range, Manchester. Although he was offered a lectureship at Mansfield College Oxford, he decided to take up his first ministry at the Tabernacle Congregational Church in Hanley, Staffordshire in 1878.

After our marriage, I resigned from my teaching post and so a new chapter of my life began. The early years in Hanley were very busy. Funds were raised to replace the Old Tabernacle with a new church, Sunday school and lecture hall and Thomas had taken the decision to act as his own clerk of works. We were keen to encourage the younger members of the church and membership quickly increased. The parsonage was the centre of many activities and gatherings.

Relatives from abroad came to stay and other ministers came to call on us. One visiting minister was General Booth, the founder of the Salvation Army, a man whose ideas were to influence our own thoughts on social reform. I enjoyed these meetings and kept myself busy supporting my husband and visiting the poor of the parish. I was keen to share my happiness with my friends in Bradford, sending them a plan of the house and telling them that I had the best husband in the world.

Very soon I was to start on a new phase of my life - as a mother. In 1880, a year after our marriage, our first child Mary Kingsland Higgs was born. Two years later, I gave birth to our only son Arthur Hilton Higgs.

As lovers of the countryside, we sometimes felt the need to escape the confines of the town and often visited nearby Trentham Park with our children and Thomas enjoyed fishing in the River Dove. Occasionally we were able to spend a holiday in the Lake District, where we had been for our honeymoon.

In 1888 I gave birth to our third child, Margaret Dorothy. Unfortunately, I became seriously ill and the doctor was very concerned about my delicate chest. Fearing what had happened to my father, he advised me not live in a smoky place. Taking heed of his words, we spent some time in Scotland staying with friends to aid my recuperation. Whilst we were in Scotland Thomas was offered the position of minster at the Congregational church in Withington,

Manchester. When my health improved, we moved to Manchester and we soon settled into our new environment. We were delighted when our elder daughter Mary gained a scholarship to Manchester Girls' Grammar School. In 1890 at the age of 36, I gave birth to another daughter, our fourth child Mabel Paddon. Unfortunately, our time at Withington was overshadowed by more health problems. Shortly after the birth of Mabel, Thomas was diagnosed with a nervous illness, which necessitated nine months away from the church. Following medical advice Thomas took a sea trip and ultimately had to resign his post. The family spent some of the time in the country and some of the time near All Saints, Manchester for the children's schooling. This was a very difficult time, both financially and emotionally, with a sick husband and four young children to be cared for. I put my trust in God and found that, as always throughout my life, good friends were there to help. I rediscovered my gift for poetry and was able to endure the dark days.

Another change in my life was about to occur. When Thomas had regained his health, he heard that a minister was needed at a church in Greenacres, a district of Oldham in Lancashire. He was asked to give a trial sermon in February 1891 and so impressed the committee that they were unanimous in wishing to offer him the post. I remember Thomas' words,

'I have been called to this place, Mary. It is His will. There is much to be done and, praise be, I am now well enough to take up the challenge.'

Oldham was a large cotton town nestling in the foothills of the Pennines, to the north east of Manchester. Greenacres Congregational Church played an important part in the lives of the local people, providing not just spiritual and moral guidance, but also education and social activities.

A month later, we moved into the large stone parsonage. It was about ten years old and the rooms were large and airy, but rather cold. The last parson's wife had borne children there and I knew it would make a happy home for our family. I read what a previous parson had written when he first visited Greenacres 40 years earlier.

The bleak and barren aspect of the surrounding district was rendered still more cheerless by the prevalence of strong easterly winds and

clouds of dust. I soon found, however, that though the surrounding hills presented a somewhat stern and inhospitable appearance, there were warm hearted friends connected with the cause at Greenacres.'

Moving to Greenacres was the start of a new chapter in my life. I was to grow to love those 'stern' hills and the warm-hearted people. I had planned to be a sort of curate for my father. His untimely death prevented this and our years at Hanley and Withington were somewhat marred by ill heath. As Thomas had said, there was much to be done in Greenacres, and I could not wait to rise to the challenge. Oldham was a damp, murky place. It was also windy, being high above sea level. As the town grew, people came to find work in the cotton mills and the mines and iron works that powered them. By the 1890s industrial buildings and terraces of stone and brick houses crowded into the landscape around Greenacres Moor, their chimneys belching black smoke into the atmosphere. Yet Greenacres cemetery, opened in 1857, rests between the parsonage and most of the houses and to the east are the hills and valleys of Saddleworth. Greenacres was not as overcrowded as Oldham town centre.

Reverend Thomas Kilpin Higgs

**Greenacres
Congregational
Church**

**The Parsonage was
built in 1880**

PART 2 - ANNIE

Chapter 3 Poverty in Oldham

I first met Mary Higgs (nee Kingsland) when her husband came to give a trial sermon at our church in February 1891. The previous minister, Rev. Thompson, had resigned due to ill health and we were eager to have a replacement as soon as possible. The sermon was well received and Rev. Higgs became our minister at Greenacres Congregational Church Oldham in March of that year. Rev. Thomas Higgs was in his early 40s and taller than most of the local men. He became a popular minister whose sermons inspired the congregation to think about social questions.

His wife Mary was about 37. She wore her dark hair parted in the middle and fastened back and her clothes were sensible rather than fashionable. She was well educated and had four children. I felt that the difference in our background, I was unmarried cotton operative, made it unlikely that we would be friends. In those early days, I could never have imagined that one day she would ask me to join her in daring undercover investigations.

When Rev. Higgs brought his family to Oldham my parents and younger brothers had moved back to the Midlands. I was working at Greenacres Mill on Huddersfield Road and boarding with my friend and workmate Edith, and her younger sister Emma. Most families in Oldham were dependent upon the cotton trade. Only a year after the Higgs family had moved to the town, they were to see real hardship amongst the local workers. Oldham had its own stock market, which started to fall in 1890, continuing downwards for the next two years. The investors were unable to meet demands and this was particularly true of the share-owning operatives and other small shareholders. As the price of the shares fell, the majority of mill owners wanted to reduce wages by 10%. Not surprisingly, the workers rejected this. The employers failed to agree on a proposal of reduced hours and the workers representatives, the Operatives' Association, refused to accept the revised reduction of 5%. After a number of meetings, the employers closed down the cotton mills locking out the workers in October 1892.

At the start of the lockout we had no idea how long it would last. Trade Unions gave their members some financial support. For example, the Card and Blowing Room Association paid each man two shillings and six pennies per week, with three pennies for each dependant child under ten. Women were paid two shillings and junior females got one shilling and six pennies. I was fortunate that I had a married sister to help me. My elder sister Eliza and her husband James lived nearby and insisted that I join them for a meal each day. They had three children so Eliza was not working. However, as James was employed in the iron works, he was not affected by the lockout. In return I was happy to help with some household tasks, as I was free during the day and enjoyed the company of my sister. Like most housewives, Eliza kept to a strict regime. Monday was washday. Water had to be heated and put into a large tin tub in the yard. After I had scrubbed shirt collars and cuffs, the washing was added to the hot tub. I enjoyed pummelling the clothes with the posser. The wooden disc on the end bashed the water through the clothes, removing the dirt. I lifted the long wooden handle (like that of a yard brush) and with two hands pushed it down as hard as I could, squashing the washing and seeing dirty water rise above it. After the washing had been rinsed, we had to remove as much water as we could. A mangle stood outside and was something that was often shared with neighbours. It was easier with two of us to lift the heavy washing and guide it through the wide rollers. I turned the handle on the right to squeeze out the water as the washing fell into another tin tub. If the weather was dry, it would be pegged out. I remember a damp November day during the lockout, when the washing had to be dried indoors. A rack was let down from the ceiling so that we could hang the washing on the thin wooden slats. Then it was hoisted up so that the heat from the fire could dry the clothes.

'Look, smoke,' cried three-year-old Charlie as he watched steam rise of the wet washing. Eliza smiled indulgently at her youngest son, and I felt happy to have close family living near me. Others were not so fortunate. The lockout put a huge strain on working

Wash tub   **Mangle**

families. The Oldham Relief Committee found that many families could only afford one meal each day. Large companies, political organizations and Sunday schools did what they could to help. Rev. Higgs and his wife Mary, whom I first met when Rev. Higgs came to give a trial sermon at our church in February 1891, gave support and encouraged others to do the same. We at Greenacres were proud of the fact that the young people of the parish gave what money and help they could. On Christmas Day 1892, our church members provided breakfast for an incredible 470 needy children. What was left over we used to provide supper for neighbours. I feel sure that this helped to keep many people alive, particularly vulnerable children, at this very difficult time.

The Higgs family had seen at first hand the poverty and even homelessness, which loss of earnings could cause. The lockout of the cotton workers is described in the church manual (yearly report) as, *'the cloud of adversity which is passing over this town and district'*. The writer goes on to describe the way in which the young people of the parish were encouraged to give their time and effort to prevent many children from having to go without food.

'Whilst this shadow, dark though it be, is resting over us, it brings with it some compensation in the manifestations we see of widespread generosity and sympathy. And in relieving the distress, we rejoice to see our young people taking so willing and active part in visiting from house to house, and providing free breakfasts and dinners for the poor children in the district every week.'

The lockout lasted 20 weeks and three days and caused losses not just to the manufacturers and the operatives, but also to the wider community. After a bitter struggle, a compromise wage reduction of just over 2.9% was finally agreed in March 1893. Many of the congregations were working-class and according to the Higgs' eldest daughter, her own family was not well off. Mary Kingsland Higgs, who would have been 13-years-old in 1893, later recalled the difficulties.

'It was a life of almost Franciscan poverty at the Parsonage with four children growing up and the cotton trade none too prosperous. Other people's poverty was more pressing, for in 1893 there was a long cotton strike and the poor needing relief came constantly to the Parsonage, where sympathy was never lacking.'

The yearly salary of the minister was £200. A great deal more than the average working man, but most working men had other family members in employment adding to the total household income. Obviously, it was not be socially acceptable for a minister's wife to have paid employment. Rev. and Mrs. Higgs encouraged their children to continue their education well past the age of 11 which limited any further contribution to the household income. Certainly, the family would not be wealthy by middle-class standards and Mrs. Higgs later spoke of 'financial restraints' when the children were young. They usually had to spend the school holidays at home and Mrs. Higgs enjoyed taking her children to the countryside around the town. Rev. Higgs was a countryman at heart, being brought up in the Suffolk countryside. He enjoyed outdoor pursuits such as gardening, fishing and sailing (not something he could easily do in Oldham) and playing cricket. He cleared an area of rough moorland near the parsonage to make a garden and encouraged others to do the same.

The idea of creating gardens from rough ground was something that Mrs. Higgs was to expand into something far more ambitious at the beginning of the next century.

As a minister's wife, Mrs. Higgs soon became involved in many church ventures, especially those involving young members of the community. She had a friendly, no-nonsense approach to life and was eager to settle into her new home. Like me, she taught a Sunday school class and that is how I first got to know her. One Sunday, as I was about to leave after class, she spoke to me.

'What's your name, my dear?'

'Annie, Mrs. Higgs.'

'Were you born in Oldham?'

'No, Wolverhampton, Mrs. Higgs.'

'I didn't think you were born in this town. Please tell me more about yourself and your family.'

'Well, my father's an insurance agent and he brought us here, um it must be about 24 years ago. I'd be about six years old.'

I tried to speak clearly and without dialect words when talking to those who were my 'betters' and smiled at the fact that she had recognized that my accent not a 'pure' Oldham one.

'Did you enjoy school?' She asked.

'Oh yes, I did. Though when I was 11-years-old, I started to work half-time in the Clarksfield Mill in Ogden Street. Some weeks I walked there in the morning with my elder sister Eliza and then went to school in the afternoon. Other weeks I worked in the afternoon after school. Some of the pupils were so tired they fell asleep in class, but I was keen to learn and usually managed to keep awake - just. Even when I became a full-time cotton worker I continued to study, going to night school on two weekday evenings each week. I also went to Sunday school at the Congregational church. There was a separate room for the "select class" where I was trained to be a Sunday school teacher.'

I finished by telling her that, as a single woman, my social life revolved around the church.

'It looks as if we will be spending some time together, so please call me Mary.'

I felt a little uneasy about it, but I was soon calling her Mary and getting to know her children. The eldest child was named Mary

Kingsland Higgs (Kingsland being her mother's maiden name). She was about 11 years old and a pupil at the girls' grammar school in Manchester, where the family had lived before coming to Oldham. She had fair hair and steady eyes and was a studious child, rather mature for her years. The second child was a boy – Arthur Hilton Higgs. Arthur would have been about nine and very much a lad, liking to be outside rather than at his studies. Margaret Dorothy Higgs was a lively three year old who was very popular with the older parishioners. Lastly, there was little Mabel Paddon Higgs, only about a year old and just taking her first unsteady steps on her short sturdy legs. All the children had quite different personalities, but I was to become very fond of all of them. I was impressed by Mary's teaching at the Sunday school. When I made a comment, she told me that she had been a teacher at a grammar school before her marriage. She initially taught her own children at home and told me that she intended to take an active interest in the schools at Greenacres. The elementary school, also known as a British Day School, catered for children up to the age of 11 and was widely regarded as the best in the district. In 1893 there were over 300 pupils on the register, which included my sister's two lads. There was no fee for infants, but those in the first standard were charged one penny and those who had reached a higher standard paid two pennies. There was also a grammar school, which was connected to the Sunday school by a staircase. A library was set up there to encourage reading. I was not the only one to make use of it, because during 1894 well over 2,000 were circulated.

The following Sunday, when we had finished classes, Mary told me that she thought the words of the bible should be simpler for ordinary working people to understand.

'When we were on honeymoon in the Lake District, a farmer asked me why it could not be written in plain English. What do you think?'

'I agree that the language is very difficult to understand, but isn't that just how it's written?'

'It causes confusion and even distress.'

I was unsure about this.

'How do you mean?'

'When Arthur was about five years old, I was reading to him and he became quite frightened by the idea of the Holy Ghost.'

'Yes I see,' I said, not sure if I should smile at this.

'You know young Nellie in my Sunday school class?'
'Yes.' I pictured the tiny mill-lass scrubbed clean in her Sunday clothes, her thin mousy hair scrapped back from her high forehead, making her grey expressive eyes look even bigger.
'She was slowly and carefully reading from Matthew 6.

Take heed that ye do not your alms before men, to be seen of them: otherwise, ye have no reward of your Father which is in heaven.

I thought that she might not have understood the lesson, so I asked if she knew what it meant,' said Mary.
'Yes Mrs. Higgs' replied Nellie, holding up her bony little arms, 'Ah shouldn't show these t'men.'
Mary said that she found it hard not to smile realising that Nellie thought it was a lesson in modesty. This time I laughed aloud, as I pictured Nellie's innocent expression and 'Some of the words do cause a lot of confusion,' I said.
'The language needs to be changed so that those with limited education can understand the scriptures.'
I agreed, but was amazed by what she said next.
'I have started to translate the New Testament into plain English.'
I did not reply.
'But not from the King James version, from the Greek.'
I was even more taken aback. Here was a woman who understood Greek, a woman who could even consider the task of translating the bible. All this was beyond my grasp.
Throughout her life, Mary led by example. Initiating the translation of the New Testament was one of the first schemes I knew about. She made a start on the first two chapters of St. Mark's Gospel from the Greek. This meant she had to 'brush up' on the language.
At Greenacres Church there were a number of classes and groups to join. In my younger days, I had attended the Young Ladies' Class with my sister. Rev Higgs and his wife were keen to set up other groups where our skills were put to good use.
'Can you sew, Annie?' asked Mary. 'Yes, I learned at night school. I can do plain and fancy hand stitch and use a sewing machine.'
Mary said she was delighted as she was starting a sewing group.

'Come along next Monday night at 7 pm. Oh and bring anyone else who you think would like to join us. I'll set the room up for 12.'

The following Monday I arrived early, armed with my sewing basket and accompanied by my friend Edith.

'Ah, do come in Annie, and this is?' asked Mary motioning towards my friend.

'This is Edith, Mrs. Higgs. We work together.'

'Can you use a machine, Edith?'

'Yes, and I can do plain and fancy hand sewing,' replied Edith with enthusiasm.

The room had been set out with a treadle machine, two hand machines on small tables, and a large table in the centre with wooden chairs around it.

Mrs. Crabbe, a woman about 50 came in with two younger women.

'Hello Mrs. Crabbe,' said Mary.

'And these must be your daughters.'

'Yes, this is our Miriam and our Molly.'

Mrs. Crabbe had brought a large piece of flannelette.

'That's wonderful, Mrs. Crabbe.' said Mary.

Mrs. Crabbe, a widow, was a well-respected member of our congregation. Miriam was a few years younger than me, I would say in her mid-20s and Molly was about 17-years-old. Two more women came in and we all sat around the large table. Before long the room was full. Mrs. Crabbe had cut up materials and we were busy chatting while making undergarments and nightclothes for the neediest children of the parish. From then on we met each week, repairing clothes from jumble sale leavings to give to the many women who came to the parsonage for help. We also helped mill girls to alter clothes for work.

At Greenacres there were also groups to encourage young men to become involved and to keep them from the ale house and other temptations. A year after the Higgs family arrived, the Greenacres Young Men's Social Club for over 16s was formed with 59 initial members. Mary began teaching the Young Men's Class. This was not strictly for young men as any man over the age of 16 could attend, and many were not exactly young.

Mary had a much better education than anyone I knew. She told me that she was one of the first women to be educated at Cambridge.

Consequently, she was able to communicate with educated men and indeed met many prominent figures during her life. Still, she had the common touch and was able to talk to even the poorest in the district. The woman I grew to know radiated warmth. Her persuasive and optimistic manner won over many people. Therefore, I was shocked to find that she was not always a happy soul. It is clear from her honest words that she found the responsibilities of caring for a young family very tiring and sometimes tedious when she wrote,

'Yet wings are clipt, flight is scarce possible, the past is lost.
Life is not what it seemed, but a slow progress under daily care that rests as constant burden, pressure of necessity.
How can the past survive? Were dreams untrue?
Is daily life narrowed to menial task, mere food and clothes?
Time fails 'mid mother duties to renew and feed the life of mind, the lamp of soul burns low, the oil of love comes but in driblets, what remains?
Shall life itself ebb out, so great the strain?'

It seems likely that she was thinking back to her time as a privileged student when anything seemed possible and comparing that with the constraints and strains of motherhood.

The Sunday school at Greenacres. This building was begun in 1889 – the tender was for £1,740 – and opened in 1890. In addition to religious instruction, the new Sunday school was used for tea parties, lectures and large meetings.

After leaving school, most girls in Oldham found work in the cotton industry, until their first child was born. A few still continued, and babies were brought to the mill to be fed, or left with a nurse mother. There were more women than men so, like me, some remained unmarried and continued to work in order to support themselves. Working-class women, especially unmarried ones, were finding that they could become involved in things outside the home. In the workplace, some women had become interested in trade unions and politics and wanted more say in things which affected their lives. The Independent Labour Party was founded about 1893 and in Oldham women like cotton worker Annie Kenney circulated socialist publications around the mills. Annie was the first woman to be elected to the local committee of her union, The Card and Blowing Room Operatives and would later be a prime mover in the fight for women's votes.

In nearby Rochdale, another woman was working to improve social conditions. Jennie Wareing, an ex-cotton weaver, became the Northern representative of the Christian Endeavour Society. This Society helped young people from industrial areas to have some time away from home in the countryside. Mary Higgs met Jennie at a meeting of the Society in Liverpool. Mary was so inspired by the work Jennie was doing, that she founded an Oldham branch of the Society. Despite the difference in their education and class, the two women became firm friends. Some years later, Mary was asked, by one of the many young people that Jennie had helped, to write Jennie's biography. It is unusual to have biographies written about working-class women, so Mary must have been very impressed by what Jennie had achieved. The book was published under the title *Mother Wareing*.

At the end of 19th century, opportunities to extend education had improved. Mill workers like me could go to night school classes, which were often connected to a local church. For those whose family did not rely on their wages, educational opportunities were slowly increasing. The Higgs' eldest daughter, Mary, had started at Manchester Girls' Grammar School when the family lived in Withington. She left around 1898 aged 18 after gaining a scholarship to Westfield College. The headmistress was Constance Maynard, whom Mary knew from their days at Girton. The two younger daughters, Margaret and Mabel, went to Hulme Grammar School for Girls which opened in Oldham in 1895.

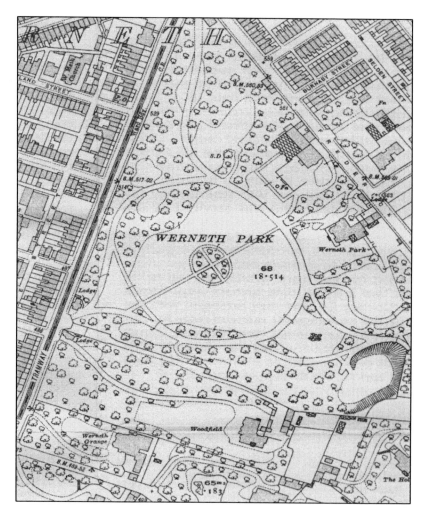

Wealthy mill owning families built property at Werneth. Woodfield (centre bottom) was owned by the Emmott family and the Lees family owned Werneth Park which was situated just off Frederick Street.

Chapter 4 Mary Finds her Sphere

When Mary came to Oldham, her children were aged between 11 and one, so were still dependent upon her. She was eager to share her knowledge and ideas with others and started to give talks around the town, but vowed only to speak at places near enough for her to be back home by early evening. As her children grew, she became increasingly involved in schemes and projects around the town. More avenues were slowly opening up for women, especially those who did not have to work. In 1895 the National Union of Women Workers, later known as the Nation Council of Women, was founded. Two years later, a meeting was held at Woodfield, the Werneth home of Mr. and Mrs. Emmott with the intention of forming an Oldham Branch. Alfred Emmott was a local cotton manufacturer who had enormous local influence (Mayor of Oldham 1891 and 1892 and MP from 1899). Present at the inaugural meeting were Mary Higgs, Sarah Lees and her two daughters Marjory and Dorothy. Mary Emmott was elected treasurer, Sarah Lees was elected president, and the six vice presidents included her daughters and Mary Higgs. Sarah Lees was the widow of Charles E. Lees, a wealthy mill owner and son of Eli Lees. When Charles and Sarah married, Eli made his house at Werneth Park over to the couple. Charles died in 1894, leaving most of his considerable estate to be divided between Sarah and her two daughters, allowing them to finance worthy schemes. Mary Higgs was to be an instigator of many of their future social initiatives. Marjory later wrote about their relationship with Mary. *'It was at the turn of the century that we formed a life long friendship with that remarkable pioneer Mrs. Mary Higgs.'*

There was a mutual respect and Mary described Sarah and Marjory as women whose *'price is above rubies'.*
The Oldham Branch of the National Union of Women Workers discussed such topics as: emigration, infant mortality, care of the 'feeble minded', public health, wage-earning children, working conditions of women, women in public work and women's suffrage. They actively campaigned for improvements by giving talks and writing letters to newspapers and those who could effect change. For example, women and girls who worked in shops, restaurants and

hotels were often exploited, unlike the mill workers who had some regulation of their hours and wages due to trade union pressure. The NUWW called for the hours to be 'within the limits similar to those permitted in factories'. They also stressed that young women under the age of 18 should not be working after ten at night for obvious safety reasons.

Since the industrial revolution people had moved to the towns from the countryside to find work and many now lived in cramped, unhealthy conditions. Some philanthropic employers were beginning to build villages and small towns of good quality houses for their workers. As a young woman Mary had taught at the school in Saltaire, a small town created by mill owner Titas Salt. In 1893 another 'model village', as these communities were known, with good standard housing and open spaces, was created by the Cadbury brothers at Bournville in the Midlands.

Ebenezer Howard

Around this time Ebenezer Howard created the ambitious Garden City Movement. He wrote *Tomorrow - a Peaceful Path to Real Reform*, published 1898 and re-issued later as *Garden Cities of Tomorrow* and travelled around giving inspiring talks on his plans for the integration of countryside and industry. This resulted in the creation of Letchworth and (later) Welwyn Garden Cities, to the north of London. Rev. Higgs was impressed by Howard's vision, so invited him to give a lecture at our church. I heard his talk and like the Higgs, I agreed with his ideas. In fact Mary was so inspired that she was one of the first members of the Garden Cities Association which was founded in 1899. A few years later she was the prime mover in the creation of a garden suburb in Oldham. Howard stayed overnight at the parsonage and discussed his ideas further with Rev. Higgs. Mary explained the middle-class convention of the time. If a couple came to visit, men and women would split up after the meal. Men would go to another room to smoke and talk and maybe have a drink. When a man came alone to the parsonage, the men would have their conversation and Mary would sit in the corner with her sewing basket, listening to the exchanges. I got the impression that she thought that this was a privilege but I found it hard to picture this well-educated woman sitting quietly in the corner with her sewing.

Another influential man who came to speak at the church, and who stayed at the parsonage was William Thomas Stead, a Congregationalist and a champion of social reform. He was already known to Mary as a governor at the school in Bradford where she had been a teacher. Stead was an investigative journalist who became editor of the Pall Mall Gazette. He had become famous, or some would say infamous, for his exposé of child prostitution in London's brothels. He wanted to show that it was quite easy to buy a child for that purpose, so decided to pose as a customer. Members of the Salvation Army and an ex prostitute helped him to 'buy' a 13-year-old girl, Eliza Armstrong. Her mother, whom Stead fervently believed knew that her child was being sold into prostitution, was given money and the child was taken. In 1885, Stead published articles about the episode in the *Pall Mall Gazette* under the title *The Maiden Tribute of Modern Babylon*. Some critics claimed that this was sensational journalism and that he was creating news rather than just reporting events. It certainly sold newspapers! Eliza's father, a chimney sweep, complained and Stead was found guilty of 'taking' the girl without her father's permission. Stead, Bramwell Booth of the Salvation Army and the ex-prostitute who had helped to buy the girl were all sent to prison.

William Thomas Stead

Stead spent three months in jail for the offence. However after his exposé, one of the changes in Criminal Law Amendment Act of 1885 was to increase the age of consent from 13 to 16.

At the end of the 1890s, Mary and I were present when Stead gave a talk about social reform at Oldham Town Hall. I thought he must have been a handsome man in his younger days, but I found him to be rather intimidating. He was a powerful speaker, and it was impossible not to be inspired by his passion as he urged members of the public to become involved in the righting of many social wrongs of the day. The care of the needy could no longer be left to individuals and charities, but should be a communal duty and individuals must see that the duty be carried out. Mary agreed with his sentiments and was so impressed by his arguments that she vowed to become involved. Her husband, who had participated in the foundation of the League of Social Service, a forerunner of today's Social Services, encouraged her to stand as a Poor Law Guardian. Most guardians were men, but it seemed very important to have women to oversee the care of other women and children who were admitted to workhouses. Mary told me that the first female guardian had been elected in 1875. She was very keen to have this position at our local workhouse but said that, 'Oldham was not at the time enlightened enough to elect me.'

Although she was disappointed, this did not stop Mary. She found another way to become involved in the same cause when she became secretary of the Ladies' Committee, which visited the Workhouse in Oldham. Not surprisingly, many of the committee were already known to Mary. The chairman was Mary Emmott, and Sarah Lees and her daughter Marjory were committee members. Mary used her scientific background to develop a way to collect data.

Oldham Union Workhouse, Rochdale Road

She devised a form to record information given by the women who came to the workhouse. As a result of this, was able to collate evidence of the experiences of women in workhouses around the country. This was later to lead Mary to embark on undercover investigations.

In addition to her efforts at the workhouse, Mary was able to help needy girls and women who did not want to go there.

Although the parsonage was a little out of town, homeless women often made their way there. I helped Mary to find clothes and somewhere for them to sleep. They often arrived with just the clothes they stood up in, and many had a small child in tow. We used the leavings of jumble sales and appealed to parishioners for unneeded articles. The sewing group was always kept busy making, mending and altering. However, we could do nothing about boots, which were very difficult to come by. Mary soon realised that more needed to be done to help those women who found themselves without a place to sleep. Initially, she secured a room in the house of the widow, Mrs. Crabbe. Mrs. Crabbe, provided bed and bedding, a box for a change of clothes, a bath, towels and soap. A weekly sum of about five shillings was charged for the use of the room and the trouble involved. This arrangement was soon seen to be inadequate for the numbers that needed help. Mary was fortunate to have wealthy and influential friends. After discussing the problem with Sarah Lees, Sarah agreed to financially support the acquisition of a cottage in Esther Street off Greenacres Road. The 'little rescue home,' as Mary called it, was set up around 1898 and I was proud to be asked to play a big part in this enterprise. Mary asked if I would be willing to live in the house as a sort of matron. Mrs. Crabbe's daughter Miriam, a cotton weaver was also asked to help. So Miriam and I, under Mary's instructions, set about organizing the 'home' and making it ready to take in women who needed our help. The house was a typical brick terraced two-up, two-down with a small back yard. The backroom had a fire that heated the room and water. The oven at the side could be used for cooking, but there was also a gas stove. Cupboards were built into the alcoves, with shelves above for pots, and a stone sink which also had a shelf beneath, stood under the window.

Esther Street 'rescue home' Greenacres

I scrubbed the oilcloth and put a rag rug in front of the fire. Mary managed to get some old chairs and an oak table. I covered the table with a chenille cloth during the day and placed a potted geranium in the middle. I set about making curtains out of old material. There were pretty ones for the windows, a heavy weight one for the bottom of the stairs and a small one to cover the shelf beneath the sink. Half height lace curtains were also put across the windows for privacy. Miriam and I shared the front room, or parlour as it was often called. It had a small fireplace, a tallboy cupboard, my sewing machine, two beds and a couple of chairs. That left the two upstairs rooms for our 'guests'. Outside there was a tippler toilet, a 'coal hole', and a large metal tub and a ringer for doing the laundry. A tin bath hung from a nail on the wall. This was a fine time for me. I gave up work in the cotton mill and had board and keep and a small income in return for my work at the 'home.' Miriam continued to work in the mill and helped out in the evenings and weekends.

A new century dawned. The translation of the New Testaments was completed between 1898 and 1901 and published in three parts. Mary had soon realised that the task she had begun was too much for her alone. She wrote to William Stead and he agreed to print her appeal for help in his publication. Fortunately, enough people came forward. The Westcott and Hort text of the *Greek New Testament* was used and two well-known scholars of the time, J Rendel Harris and Richard Francis Weymouth, volunteered to advise the group. The aim, according to the preface was: 'to do for the English nation what has been done already for the people of almost all other countries – to enable Englishmen to read the most important part of their Bible in that form of their own language which they themselves use.' The final revised edition was published in 1904 as:

A Translation into Modern English Made from the Original Greek. By a Company of Twenty Scholars Representing the Various Sections of the Christian Church.

Writing to a friend, Mary was happy to have found a way to use her intelligence and education to start what she viewed to be a worthy enterprise, while her children were young.

'God trained me in the making of the Twentieth Century New Testament to understand how He could combine all sorts of conditions of men, bending them to His will, if they gave Him even an inch of their inner being to be directed.'

Mary continued to keep herself busy with the work of the church and helping destitute women, but she still found the time and energy to give her attention to trying to improve the local surroundings. When the mills closed for the annual Wakes holiday, families who could afford it went to the sea-side. I loved going to St. Anne's and Southport, but the most popular place was Blackpool. The stations were full of eager families waiting for a chance to breathe the fresh sea air. For those who couldn't get away, a Wakes fair was held on the market ground in the centre of Oldham known as Tommyfield. There were merry-go-rounds, side shows, steam organs and stalls to buy treats such as toffee apples. I enjoyed this but also liked to walk in the hills around the town. Like me, Mary had grown fond of the bare hills and moorland that rose from the edges of the town.

There were many places around the town to escape from the grime and smoke. During the school holidays, Mary's family was rarely able to afford to get away, so she took the children to explore Oldham and the surrounding countryside

One sunny day in August 1901, I went with her and the two younger daughters on a walk to Hartshead Pike - a monument that stands on high ground - giving good views of Oldham and Ashton.

'I have always encouraged the children to imagine what the town had looked like in the past.' Mary told me when we stopped for a rest and a bite to eat.

Turning to Dorothy and Mabel she pointed out the mills of Oldham in the distance.

'Look at the giant mills, each larger than his brother.'

The children took in the scene.

'Take in each feature and allow your mind to slowly reconstruct what it would have looked like from a bird's eye view. Can you see the church? Imagine the scene with no mills, just farms with their animals and farmhouses.'

'Yes,' said Mabel who had closed her eyes, 'I can see it.'

Mary talked about streams, cottages, and the plants that must have grown before the town was engulfed in smoke and grime. Turning to me she said, 'Surely, much could be done to create a more attractive town. A germ of an idea has been growing in my mind for some time. Thomas likes gardening and has cleared rough ground near the parsonage to create a garden. Some other parishioners have seen this and managed to do the same. Why can't we have more of this in the town?'

'It's not easy to grow things in Oldham. It's damp and smoky and then there's the high altitude,' I ventured.

'Well, yes, you're right, but I've been thinking about this and believe I have many constructive ideas on how to set about making valuable changes to the appearance of our town.'

In December 1901, an article was published in the Oldham Chronicle entitled *Beautiful Oldham! Why Not?*

Why not indeed! Mary chose that title, as she knew it would catch attention. She hoped it would cause mirth among the readers. It would be difficult for many to put the words beautiful and Oldham together, so hopefully they would read on. The piece started by creating a picture of what she thought Oldham had looked like before industrialization,

'The church standing on the hill-top was surrounded by farms, each with its old farmhouse and doubtless its garden and group of trees, the straggling street of picturesque cottages with cottage gardens was backed by fields, the stream, now buried underneath ran through a pleasant valley, where nuts and blackberries were to be found while further afield every little dell had its coppice - the Coppice itself being a well-wooded hill.'

Mary was careful to praise and encourage the people of the town, saying that they like to have nice things around them and they are able to co-operate to achieve goals,

'In no other town are greater pains taken to have a clean and tidy doorstep, pavement and window-sill. Clean curtains and something pretty in the window are an ambition of every housewife.'

This pride could be harnessed to create a more beautiful environment. To give encouragement she gave examples of schemes in the town such as the small park near the public library and places where people had worked co-operatively to create gardens. She told them of how such a project had been successful in the town of Stockbridge in Massachusetts where a scheme was started about 50 years before. Trees were planted, prizes awarded and grants given to improve areas of the town.

There was a great need to create open spaces, to tidy up the hen runs with their ram-shackled fencing, to convert wasteland into gardens and recreation grounds and to plant trees in the streets of the town. She was well aware of all the objections that negative people would come up with, so was ready for them. In answer to the claim that nothing would grow, she gave examples of areas that had been improved, and plants that had been seen to grow such as the wild hyacinth and pink persicaria which had grown at Greenacres in the previous ten years. Although trees had perished, ones that were known to grow could replace them. She suggested that suitable trees, plants and window boxes be purchased wholesale and sold on at cost to groups and individuals. If there was no space, then she suggested that a flagstone in the yard be taken up, or a window box could be put up. To the cry that children would ruin the efforts, her vision was to get children involved through schools. For the apathetic, she offered encouragement and example. As to the problems of pollution, she wanted a smoke abatement society set up to tackle that problem. Not surprisingly, there were many who scoffed at the idea. Some years later, the local newspaper wrote about how the idea was received at the time.

'It seemed like sarcasm, or an elaborate piece of irony; at best it was thought by some to be a hopeless enterprise.'

It was a daunting task, but she had able support. Her good friends, Sarah and Marjory Lees were experienced committee organizers, campaigners and very well known in influential circles within the town.
They also had property at Werneth Park where events could be staged, and the finances to back up social schemes. With women like these behind the proposal, Mary felt very optimistic writing,

'If the Women Citizens of the present make up their minds to make Oldham beautiful nothing can stop them, for it is only a matter of time. The inner spirit sometime or other is seen in outward act.'

Out of this campaign, the Beautiful Oldham Society was formed. Forty members attended the inaugural meeting in October 1902 at Werneth Park when the headteacher of Hathershaw School, George Lee, was elected as secretary. The Society produced a membership card on which was set out its six objectives. Some of the objectives were what could be called civic, such as the utilization of waste areas and open spaces for gardening and tree planting and encouraging schools, mills and other public buildings to plant shrubs and flowers in any adjoining pieces of land. Some were personal and very small scale, such as encouraging householders to grow plants and flowers in window boxes. However, the main objective was to engage the young of the town by cultivating a love of nature and gardening.

The sixth objective *'to urge the erection of varied and picturesque architecture and the laying out of building plots to provide groups of cottages with common gardens or grass plot,'* was ambitious and would take a great deal of planning, time, effort and money.

These wide-ranging ideas needed a lot of organization to convert them into action. Therefore, five committees were formed with their own agendas and a detailed map was drawn. The Society bought in bulk trees and other plants that were known to have a good chance of growing in the area. These were then sold to groups or individuals at cost. As a deterrent against vandalism, bills of protection of plants were drawn up with a view to the prosecution of those who infringed them. Just as importantly, the Oldham Smoke Abatement Society was formed in an attempt to modify the polluted atmosphere.

A spring flower show was held at Werneth Park with committee members acting as stewards. The public was charged one shilling and six pennies to see the displays. In the first year there were between 50 and 60 entries of plants grown, with prizes ranging from one shilling to twenty shillings. The committee was very keen to engage the children of the town, so schoolchildren and their teachers were admitted free of charge.

Artwork for the Beautiful Oldham Society

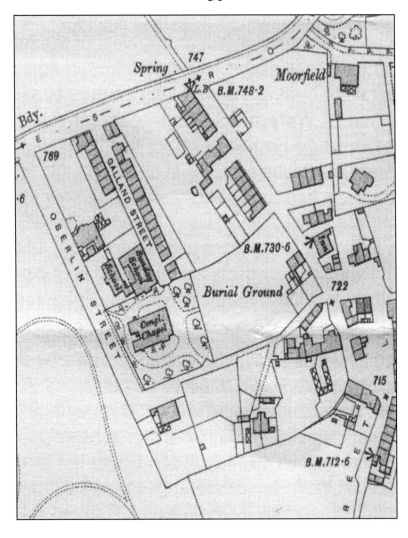

The chapel, school, Sunday school and burial ground at Greenacres.

Chapter 5 Undercover Investigations

The Beautiful Oldham Society's aims were of course long-term.
Meanwhile a constant stream of women came to our rescue home in
Esther Street. Mary continued to visit the workhouse in Oldham and I
went to the police court three mornings a week to take charge of any
woman recommended to me by the magistrates. We listened to the
stories of the women we helped and we learned that the conditions in
the tramp wards and common lodging houses were often appalling.
The common-lodging houses, we learned, were often used by
prostitutes.
'It's not so hard for a destitute woman to fall into prostitution,' we
were told. Mary was well-informed about the rules of the workhouse
and, after speaking to many unfortunate women, she knew that
changes needed to be made. Mary had collected data to use as
evidence to bring about that change but decided that this would not be
enough to convince the authorities how bad the state of affairs in the
casual wards and common lodging houses were. Something radical
was needed.
'The root principle of reform is to remove the distance between
yourself and those whose lives you want to understand,' said Mary.
She felt it was necessary to get first hand experience of the
cleanliness, the food available and the treatment of the women by
those who had been put in charge. Like most of her class, she was
concerned about the moral welfare of the women, and knew that many
turned to prostitution.
Mary wrote,

*'Having gradually been brought to the conviction, by investigation of
numerous cases of destitution among women, that there were
circumstances in our social arrangements which fostered immorality,
I resolved to make a first-hand exploration, by that method of
personal experiment, which is the nearest road to accurate
knowledge, of the conditions under which destitute women were
placed who sought the shelter of the common lodging-house or the
workhouse.'*

The social experiment Mary referred to was the courageous step of going undercover to find out what the conditions were like in the accommodation available to homeless women. She intended to take every opportunity to listen to the stories of the women she met to give weight to her own findings.

Mary was not the first person to undertake this type of investigation. I later found out that Jack London, an American writer had, under the guise of a tramp, stayed in casual wards in London in 1902 and published an account of his findings in 1903. However, Mary was the first woman, and her sex made her more vulnerable. It was not easy for Mary to persuade her husband to give his approval to the venture. He was very concerned about her safety and health, but he also believed that changes needed to be made to improve the provisions for homeless women. Mary was a determined woman, willing to put herself at risk to obtain first hand information about this important issue. So, it was agreed that Mary would set out with a woman companion. The companion was keen to remain anonymous, and Mary never disclosed her name. However many years later, I feel that Mary's story must be told and I am now ready to reveal that I was that companion. We considered what we might find. Our experience of talking to destitute women convinced us that the dirt, discomfort and the risk of illness would have to be expected but much worse than any of this was the risk of rape.

As the time grew closer I was starting to have misgivings but Mary, with her positive nature, seemed to me to be viewing this as something of an adventure. It was arranged that we would be expected at the home of her friends in Bradford five days later, having been on a 'walking tour'. We wanted to look the part, that is poor but of good character, so great care was taken with our disguise. Our clothes were well-worn and shabby but respectable. I wore a grey tweed skirt and a black woollen shawl over a blouse that had once been white. I carried an old hat and an even older shawl. Wrapped in the shawl were a towel, some soap and some other small items such as spare stockings. Mary was dressed similarly but also carried a battered umbrella.

Even in our disguise, Mary did not want to take the risk of being recognized. She was known by many people in our area and she thought that what we were about to do was probably illegal. Therefore she decided that we would travel to Yorkshire.

Late one Monday afternoon, in the summer of 1903, we took a train from Oldham to West Yorkshire to start our experiment. When we got off the train in Huddersfield, we spent some of our two shillings and six pennies on a loaf and ½ lb of butter.

'Our first night will be spent at what is known as a Model Lodging House,' said Mary.

'Well that sounds promising. Why is it called that?'

'It was converted from a warehouse about 50 years ago and it is claimed to be the only lodging house to be constructed and supported out of public rates.'

The two down-at-heel women of middle years (Mary was 49 and I was 43) arrived at the large municipal lodging house in Chapel Hill, just over half a mile from the centre of Huddersfield, around 6 pm. The lofty building looked respectable enough from the outside. The kitchen was roomy with a high ceiling and an impressive range. A stone sink stood in the corner. Nearby, wooden shelves held a selection of pans, plates and basins, but we noticed there were no cups or cutlery. At first glance, all looked reasonably clean and tidy. We were given handy hints from the other women in the room, who could see we were novices. 'The water from the tap is boiling; you can use it to brew your tea,' said one woman.

'You'll need to pay a deposit for the loan of a knife and spoon,' advised another.

'Put your provisions in that cupboard,' added another helpful woman. As instructed, we used the tap water to brew our tea. We had brought sugar mixed with plasmon, and hoped this high protein, milk substitute would help to supplement our diet. We sat on a bench beside one of the wooden tables to eat our supper of bread and butter, washed down with a basin of hot sweet tea. After we had finished we washed our pots. There was one dirty dishcloth and a roller towel which was for drying pots and hands. We decided not to use either, so put our pots away to dry naturally.

Upstairs was a sitting room with more wooden benches and tables, with the bedrooms beyond. In the dim evening light, all looked acceptable. Mary and I opted to share a bed in the married quarters, reasoning that we would be warmer and safer. This would cost us six pennies per night. Our 'room' was a boarded-off cubicle with a lockable door, but there was no-where to put clothes, except to hang them on a nail, which had been hammered into the partition. The top sheet was clean, but the bottom one was dirty, and the pillows were stained and smelly. We spread the skirt of a clean dress over the bottom sheet and pillows and tried to make ourselves comfortable, but the flock bed was hot and uneven. It was difficult to sleep because of the annoying noises made by the other couples. A man snored, others talked and a woman, described by Mary as a 'nagging wife', kept loudly telling her husband to 'shut up!'

Mary opened the window to try to get rid of the stale smell. The worst thing of all was the bugs! Even in the dim light from the window, we could see them on the walls and ceiling and we feared they would crawl over us during the night. Mary saw one crawling near her head and killed it. After a restless night, we were woken at 5 am when some men got up. Unable to get back to sleep again we decided to get up at 6 am. The morning light showed that the walls and floor were not clean at all. In the kitchen the smell of breakfasts being cooked mingled with the odour of stale sweat and tobacco smoke. How we longed for fresh air. We wanted to wash, but we could see there was a man washing his dirty pots. All personal washing, by the men and the women, was done in the kitchen sink, which was also used to wash pots and pans.

'It's impossible to keep clean in a place like this,' said Mary as she tried to wash herself while fully dressed.

'And very difficult to maintain a level of modesty', I replied noticing that a couple of men were waiting to wash. One of the women told us that there was a 'slipper bath' but that was only available at extra cost. I had never seen such a bath, so Mary described it as, 'freestanding and usually rests on four feet. The head end of the bath rises up to make the (heeled) slipper shape after which the bath is named.'

The woman in charge sat on a bench in the kitchen, smoking a pipe and talking to one of the women. She was only very young to have a position like this, no more than 23-years-old we guessed, and her language was free and often profane. Her presence would not dissuade bad conduct; in fact, Mary said to me that she thought the woman could easily be tempted by the male visitors. All this made her totally unsuitable for the job. We looked around the room. We asked some questions saying, quite truthfully, that we needed somewhere to stay the following night. We were told this place was like a palace compared to most places they had stayed in. Sleeping arrangements were compared and one woman told us of a place where eight married couples slept in one room, with one bucket, which she pointedly described as, 'for all purpose'.

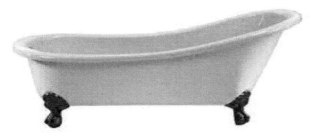

A slipper bath

There was a great deal of discussion about the insect pests that were present in most places. A woman advised us to use a hat pin to get at them from between a partition and a wall. It had been stressed that this was a fine place compared to many and we were later to find out just how true that was. Unfortunately, we were not able to get any more information because the conversation then moved to another topic. There was to be an execution that morning at 8 am and all the women were familiar with the case of the 'Moat Farm Murderer'. The women were keen to discuss the crime and the possible feelings of the wife murdering felon. They watched the clock. Mary was not happy about the conversation and was glad when the clock struck eight. The execution of Samuel Herbert Dougal took place at Chelmsford Prison at 8 am on Tuesday 14th July 1903. Therefore, without having to rely on my memory, I can pinpoint the exact date of our visit to the lodging house. We were eager to leave when the office was opened at 8 am and we were given back our deposit for the loan of the cutlery.
It was a fine morning but the grey sky threatened rain. We estimated that the next lodging house was about nine miles away. After a restless night, we needed fresh air and were glad to get out of the town. It would be more pleasant to walk along the side of the canal, or so we thought. Some men, who were working on a barge, shouted

to us in a familiar tone and asked us to join them. I had spent long enough working in the cotton mill to have heard that sort of thing, but Mary was shocked by their suggestions. Judging from her expression, she was also angry. I'm sure she would have berated the men if that had not meant moving out of character. As the wife of a minister, she was used to being treated with respect. She had not had any experience of the bold way in which many working men look at and speak to women of their own class or lower. At midday, we stopped to eat some of our bread and butter. Without a knife, it was difficult but we managed as best we could. Another tramp came to join us on the bench. She was tramping to meet her husband who was also on the road, travelling from town to town looking for work. We asked her about lodging houses in Dewsbury. We feared they would be worse than the municipal one, as there would be no regulations and would be run for profit. It was also well known to us that prostitutes frequently used lodging houses.

'Theer's two, but one's reet rough. T'other un's better. It's onth'ill up yonder.' She pointed ahead. We thanked her and continued our walk. Soon it started to rain hard. We went through the wood and tried to shelter under the trees for a while in the hope that it was just a shower. The rain continued, and as were feeling cold and stiff, we decided to walk to the town. What we needed was a hot drink and a warm room. The café sold us hot mugs of tea for 1d (one penny) each. It was such a pleasure to sit in a dry place and eat a little more of our loaf and drink the warming tea. By the time we had finished, the rain had stopped. We walked around the district and found a post-office. Mary sent a postcard home and asked directions to the lodging house. We planned to arrive there between six and seven. The lodging house was a substantial stone building that looked as though it had once been a spacious farmhouse. The stout landlady greeted us pleasantly and led us inside. This particular lodging house she told us, took married couples, those with children and single men and women. 'You can share a boarded-off compartment for eight punce,' she said before directing us into the kitchen area. Here long benches stood at each side of a wooden table. We sat down to eat our food but immediately felt uncomfortable because of the Negro sitting opposite. Although we tried to avoid eye contact, he looked us up and down. The bread and butter stuck in my throat and I was glad I was not alone. The woman who was cooking for him kindly gave us a cup of tea. Although we politely accepted it, we found it difficult to drink, worrying that we might catch something. Mary later told me that although the woman wore a ring, she doubted that she was married to the powerfully built Negro. This, she said, was judged from the conversations she heard between them. Sitting next to the large Negro was a quiet looking woman with two well-mannered children. She was busy crocheting. Also on the bench was a young man who was enjoying tossing a giggling baby into the air. The plump baby belonged to a young woman of about 24, who also had a badly behaved boy of about two-years-old, who charged around wildly, getting into mischief. Mary addressed the mother.

'What a bonny baby. What's her name?'

'Thank you missus, she's called Molly. She wer born ont'road. Me man's gone off looking fer werk,' she replied and added, 'Don't know when he'll be back.'

At the stove, a shabbily dressed old woman was cooking onions and potatoes for her blind husband. The landlady had found him a small stool to sit on, and he waited wearily with his faithful black dog at his feet. Both master and dog emitted the kind of odour often associated with old, infrequently washed bodies. In the middle of the room, a perambulator held the man's musical instruments, his only means of raising much-needed money for himself and his wife. A couple of older girls were pushing another perambulator back and forth and several young children darted boisterously about the room. There was also a great deal of noise from the people in the other part of the room. In fact, two rooms had been knocked together. Each area had a fire. The kitchen part had a sink and a cupboard as well as the stove. There were a few saucepans and pots near the sink, but nothing looked clean. Various items of clothing were hanging from a line strung across the room, close to the fire. A young woman came in and took her place on the bench. She was, I guessed, in her early 20s and quite striking to look at. Her face would have been handsome if her nose had not been so crooked. Soon she was matching the stories told by the Negro. Each seemed to vie with the other to relate the most debased tale. He told, with too much shameless detail, how he had spent the night at the house of a harlot. He had found that she hid her money in a flowerpot, so he put his there too. When she thought he was asleep, she went through his pockets. He got up whilst she was sleeping and took all the money from the pot. He took a hansom cab, enjoyed a good breakfast and bought some new clothes. That night he danced with her, but she did not recognize him as he now looked like a toff. The Negro slapped his muscular thighs and laughed uproariously at how he outwitted her. The young woman tried to compete with her story of how her nose became broken by an admirer. We did not want to hear the profane language she used to describe the way in which she had 'made him pay.' The Negro continued to try to outdo the woman with stories of his life on the seas. All this was done in a raucous tone, to rise over the level of the noise of the young children. Amid all this, one man tried to read and a baby slept. We were glad when it was time for bed and a chance for some peace and quiet, but the sleeping arrangement were not conducive to a good night's sleep. Although we had been charged eight pennies a night for a double bed in a boarded off cubicle, we found it had no door and opened on to the area occupied by the blind man and his dog. His bed was very close to ours and a rancid smell wafted our way. The proprietor had given us a candle, but there was no holder. Although the sheets looked clean, further inspection from the light of the candle, showed they covered a dirty mattress and pillows. We were unable to get to sleep, so we talked quietly about our experience. Mary was critical of many of the people who were staying in the lodging house. 'I didn't like the way the Negro looked at us with his cruel and lustful stare,' whispered Mary. I agreed that the way he looked at us made me feel very uneasy.

'I wouldn't like to be staying here on my own," I added. 'Nor I. Most the people staying here appear to be of the sort that preys upon society,' said Mary.

Downstairs someone started singing. We picked out the words, *Jesu, Lover of My Soul.* This sounded strange coming from the same mouths that had uttered such profanities. More hymns and humorous songs continued until 11 pm. Then as one, the crowd came upstairs. Such was the noise that we felt that they were closing in on us. Near by, very close it seemed, we heard the Negro and his woman, then a couple with two children, then another couple get into their beds. The only ventilation came from one chimney. It is impossible to describe the smells created by that number of human bodies, plus a four-legged one, closed into a room all night. I tried to sleep. Someone, probably a man, was scratching. A baby was suckling. Other sounds, which I will not attempt to describe and I would rather not hear, came from couples in bed together. I dozed, but suddenly woke to see a bug on the ceiling. I grabbed Mary as it landed onto the bed of the blind man. At last, I fell into a deep sleep. Mary had only been asleep for an hour or two when she felt something crawling on her. The insects were on the ceiling, the bed, the partition and heading for our clothes. She must have been horrified, but told me in the morning, with characteristic good humour, that she spent the rest of the night hunting and killing them and that she had quite a collection by the time I awoke. Again, there was little chance of keeping clean. The only sink was in a room where men were sleeping on benches, so we were only able to wash our faces and hands. Even worse, there was only one water closet for 40 people, but it was completely dry. The stench was enough to knock you off your feet. Places like this must be hotbeds of disease and some people had been there for six weeks. We had a little bread and butter left, which we had taken to our room for safekeeping. Although we didn't feel like eating, we knew we needed to keep up our strength. I washed a stained teapot and mugs and made a pot of tea. A girl of about 12-years-old, the daughter of the proprietor, was sweeping the floor causing dry dust to fill the air. We were glad to leave. How sweet it was to breathe the outside air, even though the day was dark and damp. With the two pennies we he had left, we bought a little food. Feeling jaded, we decided to spend some time in the local park. At least we could get some drinking water there. We saw a summerhouse where we thought we could find somewhere to rest, but when we looked inside, a man was asleep on the bench. It was too damp to sit outside, so we walked on and talked about the places and the people we had seen. We were very weary.

'There is one thing to look forward to at the workhouse,' said Mary optimistically.

I could not think of anything so asked, 'What's that?'

'A hot bath,' replied Mary with a smile.

Time passed slowly. It had started to drizzle with rain, but we managed to find a bench under a shelter where we could eat our food. By then cold and damp, we made our way to the free library. There were three ladies in there. One stared at us, but the others took little notice of us as we sat with our mill-shawls pulled around our bodies. It was comforting to be in a warm safe place and we managed to read for an hour or so. At last, it was time to make our way to the workhouse in Dewsbury, which was about two miles away. As we neared the workhouse, we met an old woman hobbling along. 'Hello dear,' I greeted her, 'Are you going to the workhouse?''

'Ah yam, luv. Ah've just begged a cup a tea at that 'ouse. Ah'm jiggered. Me legs er playin mi up wit'rheumatics.'

She had been in the workhouse infirmary for months and was now walking to her brother's house. He had written to tell her that she could stay with him. He was 'comfortable' she said and would give her a home. Unfortunately, she had lost the letter with the address. Therefore she must walk, staying at one workhouse after another until she found him. Her clothes were old and dirty but well mended. We judged that she was a respectable woman.

'Do you have children?' Enquired Mary. She told us that she had brought up a large family who were now all married 'Thi've enough t'do t'look after umselves.' was her resigned reply. She had not slept well due to the pain in her leg. In the morning she had lost heart and started to turn back, but rallied herself round. We wished her well and left her as she was going to another house to try to beg some food and another drink.

It was almost 6 pm when we reached the stone wall which enclosed the workhouse buildings. The sturdy wrought iron gates were supported by two stout stone pillars, which were each topped by a large gas lamp. Beyond the gates, we walked along the tree lined path to a small stone lodge that stood some way from the workhouse itself. The area around was pretty, but felt lonely, and we were glad we had not arrived alone. We could see that the door to the tramp ward stood open, but we could not see anyone. Three male tramps joined us in our wait at the lodge. Another man limped towards the door. He looked exhausted from his tramp. He was dressed in very ragged clothes and had the resigned look of the truly destitute. It was just before 6 pm that a man came out of the lodge. The three men were quickly dealt with and sent to the male ward. The lame man was refused entry. 'Ah've, sin thee afore. Tha's bin eer awready this month. On thi way now,' scolded the lodge keeper who, by the look of him, was a pauper himself. Mary and I exchanged looks. We did not think the poor man could possibly manage to walk to the next workhouse that night. He would have to sleep rough in the open. It had started to rain so we were thankful to be allowed in a few minutes early. I went in first and was asked some information about myself such as name, occupation, age, where from, where going to. After answering his questions, I was sent to the door of the tramp ward some way off. He asked Mary to go into his room. He addressed her in what she thought was a pleasant manner. 'It's a pity tha din't cum 'ere a bit earlier, Ah cud a given thee a cup o'tay,' was his friendly remark. Mary was a little confused by his kindness and wondered if he always said such things. He asked her some questions and after she told him her age and that she was married, she was shocked by what he said next. 'Just the right age fer a bit o' funning; cum down t'mi later in th'evening,' he leered. Mary was struck with dread. She was alone and in his power. The best option, she reasoned was to remain quiet but he took that as consent. Not only was this man of a lower class, he was a pauper. He took her small bundle and her last penny in exchange for a wooden token. Feeling unnerved she made her way to me. Before she reached me, I realised that I had to give in my bundle and penny. I had not witnessed what had happened to Mary, so I was appalled when I entered the lodge and the pauper tried to kiss me. It is always easy to think of a suitable indignant reply after the time has passed, but in the heat of the moment words failed me. I was shaken and pulling away, I could feel the blood rushing into my cheeks. I hurried to meet my friend inside the ward. She looked stunned. We exchanged horror stories about the pauper as we waited for the matron. Mary vowed that she would report his behaviour before they left the ward. We were, Mary said, virtually solicited and I agreed. How frightening it would have been to arrive alone. The room where we waited was oblong with six bedsteads. The mattresses were wire with no covering and the straw pillows were very dirty. A wooden table and a bench completed the furniture of the room. We walked to a low window. The bottom panes were frosted, but one had broken and been replaced with clear glass. In the yard below we could see where the male inmates broke stones during the day. Maud, our tired old tramping companion arrived and eased herself onto a bench with a groan. At last a fleshy middle-aged woman came into the room and asked the three of us, 'Are you clean?' Maud was excused as she had spent the previous night in another workhouse and said she had bathed there. Despite that, I noticed that her clothing was not clean. We made it clear that we would like a bath. In fact, it was the one thing we were looking forward to. Our own clothes were taken and locked away until morning and we were given blue nightgowns. These had plainly been worn before, as they were stained and dirty around the neck. Obviously, the inmates could have personal vermin and Mary saw several bugs on the ceiling. 'I hope they've been stoved.' Mary said as I looked at the grubby gown. We knew that heating the blankets and nightclothes to a high temperature should have killed the bugs. What we did not know was that some workhouses failed to stove clothes and blanket each day. After we had bathed and put on the soiled nightgowns, we were given four blankets each and told to make the bed. Considering that the bed was a mesh wire 'mattress' with no other covering, it was necessary to put at least one blanket under the body. Mary spread one over the bed, doubled another to lie on and used the other two to cover her body. I did the same. Our supper was brought in. To me, gruel is neither food nor drink, but something between. Oats cooked with water, and much thinner than porridge, it is just about edible with the addition of salt. Although there was a saltbox on the table, there were no spoons. It was impossible to mix the salt from the box into which many fingers had been dipped. Mary threw a few grains in and tried to drink the gruel to wash down the dry bread, but this left her still thirsty. Mary's heartfelt comment was, 'I no longer wonder that tramps beg two pennies for a drink and make for the nearest public house.' I could not stomach the gruel, so just ate a little bread. Maud, who was more experienced, had a little tea in her pocket. The assistant used hot water from the tap to brew it. Most of the gruel went down the WC. When we were alone Mary told me that the official recommendation was to serve gruel not tea. Not surprisingly, this was unpopular, as it did not quench the thirst created after hours of work. Some workhouses, she said, were allowing coffee, against regulations, because they found that the inmates rarely ate the gruel and it was often thrown around, even at each other. I had no inclination to throw it at Mary, but I could have willingly thrown the whole lot at the porter – salt and all. When the assistant returned, Mary told her about our treatment by the porter. She was very indignant. 'What a villain.

I bet he's given many a cup of tea.' She said and advised Mary to report him to the superintendent the following morning. 'I have to leave you now,' she told us, 'but I'll lock you in so he won't be able to get to you.'

She gave us a bucket in case we needed it during the night. With that, the three of us were put to bed like babies at half past six. Although the door was locked, we could hear the voice of the porter outside trying to get our attention. We lay quietly trying to get comfortable on the wire mattress. We covered ourselves with the blankets, but could not get warm. I could feel the cold, hard wire on my back. We had been given more than the regulation number of blankets. Imagine what it would have been like with just two! About an hour later we had quite a scare when the door was unlocked and a man put his head around it to see how many were in the ward and shouted, 'How many?'

I quickly called back, 'Three.'

After that we could not sleep knowing that a man had the key, especially after Maud had told us of another place in Bradford where the care of the women was left almost entirely to a man who she said, 'did what he liked with them.'

We were deeply shocked at the thought of this and vowed to avoid that place.

After a sleepless night we rose, dressed, and managed to eat a little of the gruel. When we were leaving, the superintendent stood at the door while the pauper gave us our bundles and pennies without saying a word. The next workhouse we planned to visit was about four miles away, or so we believed. We were in no hurry to get there. The Casual Ward, also known as the Tramp or Vagrant Ward, was for those who were temporarily out of work and seeking employment and needed somewhere to sleep. It was purposely as unpleasant as possible as a deterrent. The casual poor could receive shelter and food, but must work, doing the same type of tasks as those in jail, for example oakum picking and stone breaking. They were, in effect, punished for imposing themselves on the ratepayers of the district. It was raining so we sheltered in the porch of a church to rest. We talked about our experiences, the beds, the bugs and the uncouth porter. There was no reason to think that conditions would be any better at North Brierley workhouse. At about 2 pm we started our journey, but did not arrive at our destination until nearly six hours later, having walked over eleven miles. We had misjudged the distance and had difficulty finding the place; partly due to the misleading directions we had been given. The rain had seeped through the holes in our boots and our well-worn skirts and shawls were sodden. Our battered umbrella had given little protection against the downpour. The workhouse was near a reservoir, so at least something was getting the benefit from the heavy rain. At last, we tramped down the dirty lane bordered by a high stone wall and entered the hefty iron gates. It was just before eight and we had begun to worry that we might not get there in time to for the night's admittance. Sleeping rough in the rain was not something we had planned to do. The substantial stone lodge had an office for the lone man. Thankfully, he appeared to be more respectable than the last one. We were relieved that he asked us straightforward questions and told us to sit and wait for the portress. After a couple of men had passed in, and we were alone with the man, he changed his manner and became very familiar, hinting that Mary was leading a less than moral life. He immodestly told her that he thought that a married woman needed to 'sleep warm' and asked them her how she liked his 'house.' He then gave her a screw of salt as a gift.

'If a woman comes here on her own, I often share my breakfast with her,' he added suggestively. Mary understood what he was implying and felt very offended. She took some comfort in being with me, told him firmly and indignantly that we were not that sort of women, and only needed shelter on our way to stay with friends.

'But', said Mary later, 'what might happen to lone woman with such a man?'

When the official arrived she was angry at being called so late and threatened to refuse admittance, but the man told her that we had been waiting a while so she reluctantly, and with a sharp manner, led us to the bathroom. She insisted that we bathe and watched us undress before taking our clothes and giving us each a grubby, thin cotton nightdress to wear. Understandably, after taking a bath we did not feel like putting on the soiled clothes that we knew other women had worn. We were given blankets and had to walk barefoot on the cold flagstone floor to the stone cell that would be our bedroom. We opted to share, as the wire mesh beds were double. The pillow was a strange construction, being a flat, woven wire shelf raised a few inches above the mattress. Its discomforts were still to be experienced. We made this curious bed as well as we could, spreading one blanket over the mattress and pillow, doubling another for our backs and reserving two to cover us.

When we had done our best to make up the bed, we were given supper. We were hungry and thirsty having not eaten for over seven hours. The supper consisted of thick slices of bread and mugs of gruel sweetened with treacle and a spoon to share. The sickly mixture did nothing to quench the thirst that raged throughout the night. Try as we might, we were unable to make ourselves comfortable and spent a restless night locked into our cold stone cell. Mary later wrote of the experience,

'We were prisoners indeed, and a plank bed would have been more comfortable. The pillow was a cruel invention. It was impossible to place one's head upon it; the edge cut the back of your neck, even through a blanket, and the rough meshes hurt your face. We could not spare a blanket to double up for a pillow, we were cold as it was; the blankets underneath barely kept off the rough wires, and two were little enough to cover in a cold stone cell. The pillow was a torture; we finally put our heads under it and lay flat, screwed up into any position that gave ease'

In the morning, we were still not given anything to drink so had to get water from a tap, using our hands as cups. An old woman gave Mary some wet men's boots to clean and in return shared her coffee. This was a great treat as Mary was feeling a little unwell and complained to me about the sickly gruel we were given.

'Anyone with a grain of common sense can realize the effect on the system of taking this sort of stuff immediately after a warm bath, following a wetting.' She forcefully commented to me. She thought that it was bound to have an adverse effect on the health of the women who were then expected to do a day's hard physical work. Speaking of her own experience she said, 'It's produced a peculiarly loosened feeling in the skin, as if all the pores are open.'

Our clothes and boots were still wet from the previous day's drenching and there was nowhere to sit except by an open window.

We used the sill as a table for the bread and gruel. A male pauper walked by and stared in. I sharply told him to go away. Although the window would not open very wide, Mary was sure that men would use this to communicate with the women inside. We became aware of raised voices and agitated movement at a table near us. A tall, slim woman, probably in her mid-thirties, stood up and shouted that she would not eat such vile stuff and threw her bowl of gruel to the floor. Other women followed her lead, swearing and throwing gruel around. The official ordered them to sit but by this time, about eight women were standing and shouting. The workhouse master was summoned. The group of women left the room with threats that they would not work on the food given them. After a great kafuffle, three women who were identified as the ringleaders, were bundled into a stockroom and locked in until a policeman could be brought. The official then ordered a group of women she knew were obedient, to quickly clear up the mess.

When calm had returned, she gave Mary and me cleaning tasks such as scrubbing and stoning the floors and black-leading pipes. Mary said she felt weak and nauseous and I could see that she was perspiring profusely. She rushed from the room as the gruel caused her to suffer from diarrhoea.

The next task we were set was to clean bundles of the inmates' possessions in the cobweb-strewn storeroom. Moths had eaten into the clothes that had not been well-wrapped. 'This is another inexcusable system.' Mary quietly remarked to me. 'Women finish up going out with their meagre possessions in worse condition than when they came in, making it even more difficult for them to get employment. The bundles need to be properly wrapped and stored and the women given the opportunity to wash garments.'

We were given rough aprons to work in, but that did not prevent our clothes from getting soiled from the work. After only two nights in the tramp wards, our clothing was dirty, especially the sleeves of our blouses.

Mary told me that before about 1892, paupers were kept until 11 am on the day after admission, which made it impossible for a man or woman to find work on that day. Now earlier discharge was allowed if tasks had been completed. Still it was not helpful for men or women who wanted to find employment. They needed to leave early to get work. In addition, if someone was found to be sick, a doctor could admit him or her to the workhouse proper, therefore extending his or her stay.

We worked hard and had finished before noon. The official, being pleased with our work and believing that we had friends to go to, allowed us to go on our way.

I asked Mary what she thought was the worst part about her experience.

'Perhaps the using of others' dirty nightgowns was the most revolting feature in our tramp. At neither workhouse were the garments handed to us clean.'

We later learned that the three women ringleaders were taken to court and found guilty of 'behaving in a rowdy manner to the workhouse master.' As a result, they were each given a three-week prison sentence.

We had thought that we would have to stay in the tramp ward for two nights, so we had an extra night. What were our options? We could arrive at Mary's friends' a day early; find another tramp ward, but that could delay us two nights; we could not face another lodging house and it was too wet to sleep outside. By this time, we had very little money left, in fact only two pennies so we decided to pawn a shawl for two shillings and six pennies. This gave us enough money for a meal and lodgings for the night. We found a small café and ordered food. I had sausages and Mary had a buttered currant teacake. We each enjoyed half a pint of refreshing tea. Unsure where to go next, we made our way to the ladies' restroom at a station. On the wall we saw an advertisement for a Women's Shelter in Bradford and decided to make our way there. The shelter was housed in a converted mill.

The regime was more flexible than at the workhouse, with women being allowed to enter up to 11 at night. In addition to the questions we were asked at the workhouse, we also had to provide an address of where we were going next. The facilities for washing were good; deep basins with ample hot and cold water, which could be used for personal and clothing washing. Baths were available. There was even a wringing machine. We begged a bucket to soak our aching feet. Outside we were also pleased to find that WCs in the yard were clean and well flushed. The large kitchen was in the basement. There was a good-sized stove, benches, tables and shelves for pots and pans. The women were friendly and cheerful and the presence of an agreeable elderly woman helped to prevent foul language and possible brawls. Upstairs there was a sitting room with a piano and Sankey (religious songs) music sheets. Mary played the piano as best she could without her spectacles, and others gladly joined in the singing. This amused her, and she joked that her 'stumbling playing' was in keeping with her appearance of 'having seen better days!' A young woman was surprised to hear someone play the piano and asked, 'Who is she?' but nothing further was said.

Beds were available at varying prices and women were allowed to go to bed at nine, ten or eleven, but not between to cut down disturbance. We opted to go at nine. The room was large and airy and although Mary's bed was clean, mine was dirty and I saw vermin. Nor was the floor clean. Despite this, we slept well compared to other places, but we were disturbed at ten and again at eleven when women came in with children who were noisy. A similar thing happened in the morning when people got up at different times. Outside we could hear the sound of early morning trams taking people to work. After we got up, we were told to make the bed for next person. Therefore, whoever came next would be using the same unwashed bedding.

We left in the morning, our investigations finished. As we started to walk to the home of Mary's friends, we passed some workmen who addressed us in a very familiar way. The attitudes and language of the men that we encountered, both inside and in the street, was a revelation to Mary. She could not help contrasting the way in which men looked at her with the usual bearing of a man towards a well-dressed female. She had never realized before that a lady's dress, or even that of a clean respectable working-woman, was a protection. Mary wrote,

'The bold, free look of a man at a destitute woman must be felt to be realised. Being together, we were a guard to one another, so we took no notice but walked on. I should not care to be a solitary woman tramping the roads. I was used to being treated with respect because of my position in society, but I discovered that by appearing to be tramps this layer of civilized behaviour was stripped away and we were often spoken to as fair sexual game. A destitute woman once

told me that if you tramped, 'you had to take up with a fellow.' I can well believe it.'

At the end of what we called our research expedition, we had only one shilling and one and a half pennies left. This was used to transform our appearance into that of shabby tourists on a walking expedition. The rain would explain some of our dishevelment. We found a cheap shop, and bought a hat and trimmings, tie, and belt for a shilling. I put on a more respectable underskirt of Mary's over my petticoat. My hat and shawl would pass muster. Mary's new hat, tie, and belt 'converted' her into a lady! We went to a park to trim the hat with pins, which we bought for a half-penny.

Some luggage and money had already been sent ahead, so all we had to do was enjoy the park and wait for the time when my friends would expect us. We found it very amusing when Mary's friend thought they understood our need for a wash and change of clothes after our walking tour!

Chapter 6 A Tramp Ward in Manchester

Our rescue work in Oldham continued. In February 1904, Mary decided to publish a report on what we had achieved during the year in the hope that we would get some financial help or, at the very least, donations of unwanted clothes. Over the previous 12 months at Esther Street, we had helped 48 women and girls, some with children and babies. We could accommodate three girls at a time, four if really pushed. Some girls stayed only one night, but many returned. We did our best to find work for the girls if possible. Mary kept detailed records and we endeavoured to find out what the girls were doing when they had left. She found that almost half of the girls were now in service, some of the girls had to be sent on to the workhouse to have their babies, and a small number were sent on to the Salvation Army Home in Manchester, because they needed more long term accommodation. One girl married and another went to live with friends. We were in close contact with the Salvation Army and they kept us informed about the girls we sent to them. Mary still visited the workhouse in Oldham and I continued to visit police cells to take charge of girls whom we could help. We also visited common lodging houses and took care of girls who were sent to us by the RSPCC. Therefore, in addition to the 48 women who stayed at Esther Street during the year, (some more than once) we helped another 49 in some way. A further 60 women or girls who arrived at the parsonage were also helped. Mary treated each 'case' with compassion, but criticized what she saw as general low standards in the town, writing,

"The general morality of Oldham is low, and this is hard to combat. Among large sections of the population a fall is hardly considered sinful, 'it has happened before, and will happen again,' she is 'only the same as others.' It can be completely atoned for by hasty marriage, and the girl is simply 'unlucky' if this does not take place.'

This was not something that we easily could change, as it was not uncommon for working-class brides to be pregnant. Also I did not think Oldham was different from other industrial towns. However, there were things that we could do. When Mary heard of a situation in which a young girl of 14 was exposed to corrupting influences, she took steps to 'rescue' the girl. I was asked to accompany her to visit the girl who lived with 12 others in a one-bedroomed house. The house was in a court off a street in the town centre. The road was unmade and most of the houses were overcrowded and in a poor state of repair. Downstairs was a living room with a small kitchen. We asked the mother about the sleeping arrangements. We were told that Betty, the 14-year-old slept downstairs on a sofa with her mother, while on another sofa in the same room slept her sister and illegitimate child. Upstairs slept Betty's grown up sister and two brothers. This sister also had an illegitimate child and the two brothers had partners, and one of these had a child. Those five adults and two children shared the only bed. In the same upstairs room, two boys slept on a mattress.

'What can we expect?' asked Mary speaking about the girl's exposure to what she felt was a serious threat to the girl's moral upbringing. Instead of accepting the situation, Mary intervened and Betty was taken to a safe house. She felt that a lack of parental control was a contributory source of immorality.

'A girl becomes a wage earner before she is settled into womanhood. She begins "keeping company" at an incredibly early age, and her passions are prematurely awakened before self-control is developed. Her mother loses control, if she ever had it; she stays out late, and then sleeps out.'

Mary also criticised the way in which the young of the town paraded along one of the main streets in the town centre, presumably with the purpose of meeting someone of the opposite sex.

'Anyone can see at a glance that the promenading up and down Yorkshire Street, carried on by young boys and girls, must lead to many evils.'

Mary thought that 'Purity Teaching' was the answer and wrote that it was vital to teach,

'Those high ways of thinking which are a help to true motherhood? If we could spread through the ranks of future mothers a loftier idea of

the sacredness of marriage, and the sinfulness of immorality,
something might be done for future Oldham.'

The young women of the Oldham Branch of the National Union of
Women Workers felt they should do something for those Marjory
Lees described as, 'The rougher type of working girl who does not
avail herself of the opportunities offered by the churches.'
They wanted to provide what they thought were worthwhile activities
for the girls. Mary and I went to help with the singing and games and
to show the girls how make skirts to wear for work. This was well
intentioned but the young organisers found, not surprisingly, that they
had very little in common with the working girls, and said Marjory,
'had little to offer them in the way of entertainment'. The class
difference was highlighted when a group of girls were invited to tea in
the grounds of Werneth Park, the home of Sarah Lees and her
daughter, Marjory. A tent was erected with trestle tables and benches,
but the ground was uneven and one of the girls knocked over cups
when reaching for food and 'streams of tea coloured the white table
cloths.' The girls thought it was hilarious and laughed uproariously.
The working class girls were less inhibited and keen to have fun,
whereas Marjory and her friends were concerned with manners and
'improvement.'
After our undercover investigations, Mary wanted to reach those she
felt had the power to make changes. She approached the Women
Guardians' Association with her report. They agreed to publish the
damming exposé of conditions but as Mary wanted at that time to
remain anonymous, it was published under the title, *Five Nights as a*
Tramp by A Lady in 1904. The publication, which did not name the
establishments, was sent to every woman guardian and to the
chairman of every board of guardians throughout the country. This,
thought Mary, was the most effective way of 'remedying the evils.'
The report soon came to the attention of a popular newspaper, the
Daily Mail, giving her reports a very wide readership. She had
initially decided to publish anonymously because she thought that
what she had done may have been illegal. However, it soon became
clear that to reach the widest audience it was desirable to give talks
and she agreed to speak to interested parties in various parts of the
country including Bristol and London. After reading her critical

exposé, there were some, particularly guardians of workhouses, who believed that her experiences were not typical. It was argued that what she found could have been the results of abnormal conditions. The time of year was also questioned, querying if the conditions would be the same in winter. In reply she wrote,

'The story of our Tramp was a matter of public knowledge; the personal assurance of Guardians had been given that the evils mentioned did not exist. They had examined and convinced themselves that, as regards the destitute poor, their workhouses were free from blame.'

It was Mary's view that the investigations by the workhouse guardians were not thorough and that their expectations were very low. She even suggested that it would be a good idea for them to inspect places other than those for which they were responsible, though it is doubtful that any did.

'It is so surprisingly easy to become a tramp that it is strange it has not occurred to Guardians personally to test conditions by sampling each other's workhouses or at any rate by sending into them some trustworthy witness.'

Undeterred by the hardships that she had endured Mary was determined to collect more evidence, so she asked me to accompany her again. One evening in March 1904 we set off to spend a night in the casual ward of the workhouse in Tame Street, in the Ancoats district of Manchester.

We decided to have a cup of tea and a bite to eat before going into the tramp ward, but found that we could only buy a cup of tea with the money we had. So I suggested that we walk into the poorer area of Ancoats where we might get more for our few pennies. A young mother with a fretful toddler directed us to a small, cheap but clean café. We savoured the bread and butter and warmed our hands around the mugs of hot, sweet tea. It was getting chilly outside and we knew it would be sometime before we could enjoy another hot drink.

By the time we had finished our snack it was 5.30 pm. Casual wards usually allow admittance from 6 pm so we thought we would not have long to wait. As we got near Ancoats Workhouse, we saw a row of six men leaning against the outside wall and a lone woman waiting uneasily around the entrance gate. It was then that we discovered that this place did not allow admittance until 7 pm. Not wanting to wait for over an hour, we went for a short walk around the area. When we returned it was getting dark, and we were surprised to see the gates open. We walked through, but found we were in an odd, dilapidated wooden building, where we were to continue the wait. Fortunately, it was fine, as glimpses of a cloudy sky could be seen through the many holes in the roof. The damp smell made us reflect on what it would be like to wait there in a downpour. About 15 men lounged in a line along the wall. Some were talking, but others had a blank look of resignation about them. None was old and most looked like respectable working men. Only a few looked like loafers. Two women of middle age, who were talking as if they knew each other, sat on a step. A young woman was perched precariously on the handles of a wheelbarrow. We found a place to sit on a plank of wood and pulled our thin shawls around our bodies to try to keep out the draught. A few more women arrived and then a married couple followed by more men. There were now around 30 men and less than half that number of women waiting for admittance.

By 7 pm it was dark and we had become quite cold. At last a uniformed official opened the door.

'Married couples first,' he shouted. 'You women, stand o're theer,'

The applicants answered politely, but the bumptious official's tone was harsh and intimidating. He spoke with a strong accent,

'Hast tha bin eer afore?' He enquired curtly. If a woman merely replied that she had not, his bullying order was,

'Si tha dun't cum eer agin.'

He appeared to recognise one woman. Stretching his small wiry frame as tall as he could, he snarled, 'Ah've sin thee afore.' After her quiet reply he said, 'Dun't thee sauce me. What's tha doin eer?'

The woman bust into tears, 'All Ah said was that Ah hadn't bin sin Christmas.'

'Get out wi' thee,' he roared.

The woman started to object, but his raised hand stopped her. Clutching the old shawl that contained her meagre possessions to her body, she turned and walked out into the night. We stood aghast as he abhorrently abused the women before us.

'All thee women'll av t'stay fer two neets, and thi'll av t'pick three pounds ov oakum each, afore thi can leave. Good fer nowt scroungers.'

'What sort of women are we going to be spending the night with?' I whispered to Mary. He must have some knowledge of the women to degrade them this way. We presumed that, as we were obviously respectable women, we would be treated as such. It was Mary's turn. She was asked her name and age. She gave her name and said,

'I'm 50.'

'And what's tha doin eer?'

'My husband's got work in Bolton, I'm going to join him, but can't get there tonight, so I need a place to sleep. I haven't any money and I don't want to spend the night on the streets.'

Although we had witnessed his treatment of the other women, we thought we should have no problem in gaining admission. Mary was a respectable married woman on her way to meet her husband. A very reasonable request, we thought.

'Tha's no business t' bi eer imposin on t'rates.' Was his hostile reply.

'What?' Mary said incredulously.

Inflating his puny chest, he spat, 'Ah cud gi thee three months fer it.'

This time Mary did not reply. He appeared to take this as insolence, for he said, 'Ah've a good mind t'send thee off t'meet im t'neet.'

Taken aback, and angry at the injustice, Mary quickly responded with the retort, 'I wish you would!'

This made matters worse as he went on to insinuate that she was a woman of bad character. This caused Mary to blush, which made her look guilty. She became so flustered and confused that she was unable to answer his questions properly. So when asked how many children she had, she replied 'one or two', making her appear to be the sort of woman who cared so little for her children that she was not even sure how many she had! Her answers and manner had apparently upset the porter.

'Si thee dun't cum eer agin. Ah shall know tha face, and it'll be worse fer thee if thee does,' he threatened. With this, Mary was sent upstairs. I was next. After asking my name and age, he asked me why I was going around with such a bad character. When I could not answer, he told me I was no better and spoke to me as if he thought I was a woman of ill repute. When I joined her, I was so upset that I asked Mary wretchedly, 'Do I look like a prostitute?' Mary was a little calmer, but astonished by our unreasonable treatment, 'I thought that, being a respectable woman, if I were simply to state that I wanted a night's refuge, before going to meet my husband, there would be no problem.' The harsh verbal abuse was a real shock to us. Yet later Mary saw the funny side of it, relating how she had led the man to think that she could carelessly leave children 'up and down the country'. The physical trials were to prove just as bad. The tramp ward was a barn-like place on the top storey of a converted mill. It had been divided into a number of rooms; a large dormitory, a bathroom and a water closet, a private sitting room for the attendant, a storeroom and a day room. We were instructed to wait in the day room. There was no fire, what little warmth there was came from overhead steam pipes and a cold draught blew in from outside when the door was left open. A clean and stately female attendant strode into the room and told us to hang up our shawls. We were then marched, military style, to a spotlessly clean table with brilliantly polished mugs and spoons. The benches and floor had also been meticulously cleaned. The salted gruel we were given was almost thick enough to be called porridge and there was a saltbox on the table. We were each given a thick slice of good bread. We ate hungrily. 'Gruel is not so bad – for the first time.' said Mary. After we had eaten, we were marshalled to the bathroom and searched for pipes and tobacco. We felt indignant, but also slightly amused by the idea that we had concealed those things about our persons. The bath contained the regulatory six inches of water (there was a notice on the wall to this effect). We were asked if the temperature was right, given soft soap and told to wash our hair. Mary's hair was short, but I had very long hair and knew it would be difficult to get it dry. An officer stood by with towels. 'Be sharp!' she ordered. We were given coarse, dark blue, flannel nightshirts, which we could tell from the look and smell, had been worn before. 'They're like modern versions of the hair shirt,' said Mary as we pulled them over our heads. They were a most peculiar shape and only just covered our elbows and knees. Wearing these grubby, scanty outfits, we were paraded, bare-footed, through the sitting room to collect pillows and blankets from the storeroom. We were allowed a very low leather pillow, a straw one in a white pillowcase and three rough blankets. A bath, scanty clothes and a walk across cold floors in bare feet with our hair still wet, had made us start to shiver. I thought that Mary looked even colder than I was feeling. In the dormitory, we were ordered to let down a wide board that was propped up against the wall, near the water cistern. These planks were to be our beds for the night. We got into bed at 7.30 pm, having put one blanket below and two above, as directed. There followed a long night of sheer misery, because it was impossible to get into a position of comfort. We tried lying on our backs but that needed bent knees, which caused a draught. On our side, there was too much pressure on shoulders and hips. The beds were so close that I could feel the breath of the woman in the next bed on my face. 'What a hell hole this is!' exclaimed my neighbour between bouts of coughing. I looked across at Mary struggling to get comfortable in the bed at my other side. Although we were told women would only be admitted until 10 pm, some came in as late as mid-night. It is hard to describe the discomfort; the board bed, the cold room, the closeness of others and the constant noise. Each time a woman was admitted she bathed. This caused the water in the cistern to gurgle, tap and bang. Then the officer in charge noisily turned the door handle and marched her in, giving her orders in a loud voice. A board was then let down with a thud. The officer banged the door shut on her way out. How many times this happened, I could not guess. An old woman lay near us.

'Oh dear, oh deary me. What am I to do to be saved?' she groaned as she tried to settle her weary old bones into a sleeping position.

'Be quiet, Granny,' called an irritated voice, 'we're trying to get some sleep.'

'Leave old Granny alone,' another voice shouted.

The door opened again and a woman came in followed by the official.

'That's enough noise in here,'

Then addressing the newcomer,

'Now you, put down that plank and make it up like I told you. Be sharp.'

She glanced around the room,

'I'll have no more shouting in here, or there'll be trouble!'

The official noisily left the room. My heart sank as I heard the cistern starting to fill up again.

Granny got up at least twice during the night. She needed help, but groaned when touched.

'Don't be so soft,' she was told.

At last the light of morning came. The officer stomped in, telling us to get up.

'Be sharp now!' she ordered.

We washed as best we could with cold water and soft soap. I noticed that Mary had a cold, which was not surprising having heard all the coughs and sneezes in the room at night. I folded up my blankets and saw how dirty they made my hands. Although we were assured that the nightgowns and blankets were lumped together and stoved each night to kill bugs, we knew they were rarely washed and were impregnated with the stale sweat of many bodies. Each night a woman would be allocated garments and bedding worn by another on the previous night, and some of these had not bathed or removed their dirty outer clothes because they were not fit to do so.

We took our places to eat our gruel and dry bread at 6 am. The room had no fire, and we shivered as we tried to eat. Most women left the gruel and many only ate some of the bread, stashing the rest in their pockets to nibble on during the day. What a waste – most of the gruel was thrown away. There was no tea or coffee and the only water available was from the tap in the bathroom, but this tasted of metal polish and soap. Two male tramps came in with blankets that had been stoved. While the officer was not watching, they hid any bits of bread that the women had left, under their jackets.

It was time for work. Mary thought it was a good idea to offer to pick oakum, as it was a task neither of us had ever done. I was not very enthusiastic. We sat, three to a wooden bench in a cold room, with three pounds of oakum each at our feet. Oakum is old rope, some tarred and some knotted, cut into lengths. Our task was to untwist and unravel it, inch by slow inch. The rope was rough and the only tools were our fingers. I was used to handling cotton thread, but the texture of this hurt my fingers as I struggled to straighten its coarse fibres. After two measured hours, we had only done about a quarter of a pound each, so we were relieved when the officer returned and asked if we would like to be moved to cleaning. Alice was made to pick for the rest of the day. During the morning we had heard her sorry tale. She had been a silk trader, but trade was poor and she had been reduced to selling bootlaces and charring, the most menial of cleaning work. The clothes she came in were of good quality, but were well-worn and dirty from travel. She had managed to find employment in service and had stopped here for the night on the way, but was unaware of the two-night rule. After the first night she pleaded with the officer to let her go early to her work, but was refused. The officer took pity on her tears and took her to the matron. Eventually she was released and she walked as quickly as she could to the house. However, as she was much later than expected, she was told she would not be given the work because arriving late on the first day was a very poor example of her reliability. Alice was sent on her way. Forcing back tears, she wandered around and became lost, then returned to the same workhouse. At first, Alice was denied admittance because she had begged to leave early. The matron accused her of lying, but eventually relented and allowed her admission, on the condition that she stayed for five days and picked oakum for two of those. Mary and I consider ourselves good judges of character, as we deal with many poor women in our rescue work, and we believed Alice's story was true.

'This is not charity, but punishment,' said Mary when we discussed the plight of poor Alice. She vowed to work to change the workhouse rules, which contrived against those who were genuinely seeking work. During our stay, we gained the confidence of many of the women who told us about their tribulations. We were able to tell stories of other workhouses we had been to and give a little information about ourselves without lying. No one suspected us, not by our dress, our manner or our speech. Emma was a married woman whose husband, Will, was in the men's ward. She had been well brought up, but had upset her family when she had married someone they judged to be below her status. Recently, the couple had fallen upon hard times due to Will's lack of regular work and had finished up in the workhouse. While there, Emma heard that her elder sister was dying. The couple discharged themselves and walked over 35 miles, arriving just in time for the funeral. They then had to walk back. The round trip took them a week. They both looked weary and Will had a barking cough, which we could hear from our part of the building. Emma had a gentle manner and was always willing to perform small acts of kindness for the other inmates. Mary and I hoped Will would soon find employment so that their fortunes would improve. Nanny was also with her husband. Again, she had a pleasant manner and did not complain about her life. She was a steady worker who took some pride in her appearance and her work.

Women picking oakum

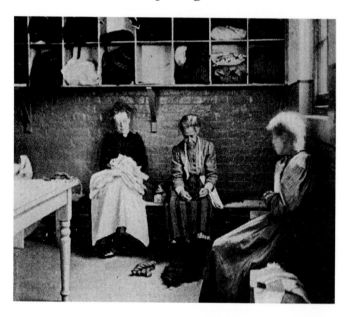

Her eyes looked tired from a heavy cold and her tramping. Before marriage, she had been a waitress in a higher class hotel in Manchester. Mary told me that she knew the place, as she had been there herself. Unfortunately, Nanny's husband had a trade that was now almost obsolete. They had tramped north to look for work without success. They now planned to tramp back again in the somewhat vain hope of finding some type of work.

Polly had been abandoned by her husband. She could have been quite pretty, but her bitterness was etched into her pinched face. She rarely smiled and her sharp tongue often let out foul language. Polly was well-known by the officials and she told us that she had been in prison for 'lip'. She told us that last time she was here; she threw bread and cheese at the officer. When she was ordered to clear it up, she swore at the matron. We thought that her attitude would make it difficult for her to find lasting employment.

At 12 noon the officer said she was satisfied with our work. Mary had scrubbed the lavatories and WCs and then cleaned the taps and stair rods with metal polish. I had cleaned the floor but found this frustrating as men continually walked past in their dirty boots. The door near our table was left ajar, causing a cold draught. After our exertions, we cooled quickly. We were given bread and cheese and were glad that a kindly officer was on duty as she allowed us some hot water. With our screw of tea and sugar we made a milk-less brew, which we shared with Granny. The old woman, known by all as Granny, was about seventy and had borne five children. She told us that her life had been relatively comfortable when her husband was in regular work. When her 'old man' had died, a son who was still at home supported her. Sadly the mill he worked at burned down. With no work they could not afford to pay the rent so they lost their home. Her son had tramped south to look for work. She could not keep up, so had been forced to beg for a few pennies, tea and sugar. She used her pennies to tip the kindly officer for hot water to make a pot of tea.

'What about your other children?' asked Mary.

'Oh, I couldn't impose on them, they have their own families to care for and I wouldn't want to be a burden'.

She had a cough and was feverish. This had not been helped by a 'treat' of whisky.

Mary spoke kindly to her and advised her to see the doctor. He examined her and allowed her to stay for a night but as she could stand and walk, he did not admit her to the workhouse proper. She decided she would try to get herself admitted the following day. She sang a hymn with Mary and then told her that she hoped she would not be long in this life.

'You may soon go to a better place,' Mary told her.

'Oh, deary, deary, me, I may go to hell.'

'What do you mean?' Asked Mary.

'I have bad thoughts about my tormentors.' by this, she meant the workhouse officials.

'If I go to hell and see them, I'll hurl bricks at them.'

I was surprised when Mary said that she thought hot bricks would be a good idea! She then suggested that Granny might think about loving her enemies.

'I don't think I can do that,' was the reply.

Mary told me that she wanted to help the old woman to gain admission, but of course, she could not reveal her identity. Also, she would have liked to have stayed with her but it would have meant standing for a long time to await entry. Although she did not like to discuss her health problems, I knew she had suffered a haemorrhage at some time. I presumed that this was after the birth of her youngest child, when she had been slow to recover. Therefore, Mary did not want to stand for long periods.

In the afternoon, we were given more cleaning chores. Mary was to scrub the floor along a wide corridor, on her hands and knees. Although she was an industrious woman, she was not used to such physical hard work. She was so tired when she had finished that she slopped some dirty water from her bucket onto the floor. I had just finished my task, so helped her to clean it up before it was seen. Unfortunately she had failed to notice that the coal box was empty, so the officer scolded her for that. I was also chided because I should have cleaned the stockroom, even though the door was locked. The officer unlocked it and I set about cleaning. Mary wanted to help but she was exhausted. Instead, she decided to sing to encourage me and others joined in. The women liked songs to remind them of home, so the Scots woman suggested *When ye gang awa', Jamie*.

After playing the women's requests, Mary moved on to hymns, which she hoped would be uplifting. We found that *Abide with Me* is a favourite amongst tramps.

The evening 'meal' was at 6 pm. We sat down in the draughty room to try to eat gruel and dry bread. After the meal, every-one sat around, weary and listless. There was no light except the skylight; there was no literature except workhouse rules; there was nothing to do except wait for bedtime.

Following a day of hard physical work, it was finally time for bed. On the second night, we were only allowed the leather pillow, which was too low for comfort. This was because the white one was only for those who had washed their hair. We were fortunate that the more benevolent official allowed us to take our shawls with us. We let down our beds and covered them with the blankets. It was good to be able to cover our arms with our shawls and try to snuggle down. However, it was still cold and uncomfortable and sleep was fitful despite our tiredness. A respectable looking woman with greying hair was to have the bed next to mine. She had never stayed in a workhouse before and I could see from her expression that she was horrified. I helped her to set up her bed. It was so close we could reach out and touch each other.

'Oh my God!' she exclaimed as she got under the blankets and tried to make her body comfortable.

At my other side, Mary started to feel sick and had to get up three times during the night to vomit. Each time she became colder.

I slept very little and woke with a severe headache, neck pains and a heavy cold. Mary looked dreadful and worried that the officer might have noticed her sickness and made her stay longer. Granny had great difficulty in putting on her tattered clothes. One arm was particularly plagued with rheumatism, so it was difficult for her to get her arm into her clothes. Then she started to swathe her legs and feet. We watched with amazement as she bandaged her feet and then wrapped old stockings around her legs and feet. When she was happy that they were protected against the cold and damp, she put on an old pair of men's boots and laced them up.

We watched Granny leave to try to gain admission to the main part of the workhouse. This was thankfully a temporary experience for us and we were very glad to be able to leave as soon as possible. Mary spoke of another woman who was forced to stay longer.

'I have family and friends at home,' said Mary, 'I pity the poor soul who has to stay for five days. This morning she woke saying she was dying of hunger. I dread to think what her condition will be at the end of her stay. And what state will her clothes be in? She will have worked in them and they are never washed. If they are stoved the heat creases them, making the wearer even less likely to find employment.'

I agreed. Despite our ordeal, I was glad that it would all be worthwhile if Mary would be able to convince those in power to make real changes that would help poor women like those we had met.

Mary wrote, 'I *felt a mere wreck. Only two days ago, I was in full health and vigour. It was no absolute cruelty, only the cruel system, the meagre and uneatable diet, the lack of sufficient moisture to make up for the loss by perspiration on two almost sleepless nights, 'hard labour' under the circumstances.'*

At the end of the visit, Mary presented her detailed evidence in a publication entitled *The Tramp Ward.* As a result, she was asked to speak at a four-day conference of the National Union of Women Workers held in York. Representing the Oldham branch, Mary dealt with the problem of unemployment from the Poor Law point of view. Getting forcefully to the point, she said that, *'The unemployed are a heritage of shirked national responsibility.'*
Equally powerfully, she went on to describe the Poor Law as, *'madness, harshness, and a national peril, penalising the destitute.'*

We had often sent girls to the Salvation Army home in Manchester and Mary was interested to see if their homes elsewhere were equally as good. When she was asked to give a talk in Bristol, she persuaded me to go with her to sample the Salvation Army home in the city. The building had been a warehouse, so the ceilings were high, making the rooms airy. A fresh-faced uniformed young woman, who called Mary 'My dear', greeted us. We were given the choice of rooms costing two, four or six pennies. So we opted for the four penny room. As it was empty and no fire was lit, the lieutenant asked us if they wanted to join the women in the two pence room, where the fire burned bright. There were clean wooden tables, benches, and shelves for a small stock of pots and pans. Unfortunately, being easily moveable, these were often stolen. It was also possible to buy food there, which was a great advantage, so we bought coffee, bread and butter for a penny, which were brought in by the officer herself. Mary said, 'That's the cheapest meal I've ever had.'
However, she found the eating habits of some women to be rather primitive. Some of the women, we learned, were long-term occupants. Two newcomers arrived. One was a beggar with her baby who had been left by her husband while he tried to find work.
The floor and beds were clean. Each wire mattress was covered with brown wrapping which could be washed. On top of this was a mackintosh, sheets and two thick blankets. Good soft flock pillows covered with white cases were provided and there were wooden boxes

into which our clothing could be stored. Although the beds were clean, Mary saw that when the women took off their outer clothing, their underclothes were dirty and ragged. She did not approve of the working-class habit of getting into bed in day clothes that had probably been worn and worked in for many days. She felt that it would better if they were removed and replaced by clean nightdresses, especially as the bedding would be used by other women the following night.

We found our treatment and the organization were reasonable and we heard no real complaints about the place or the officers. There were some well thought out initiatives; the gaslights were placed too high on the wall to be used for lighting pipes or cigarettes and the crevasses in the wall had been filled in with wood to deter insects. Mary wrote passionately about the situation in which many women found themselves, ending with a heartfelt plea for those in authority to do something about the plight of the many unfortunates,

'For here, safely folded in peace and comfort were just those whose presence on our streets is a disgrace to our civilization, and a social danger. It was abundantly evident that they were those who needed a helping hand. Few realize how terribly hard the present conditions of our social system press on women. If a girl, a woman, or worse – a mother and child – are forced to remain out all night, God pity them. Yet it is terribly hard for a woman, once down in the friendless state, with no one to speak for her, with clothing getting daily more dirty, and ragged, to obtain any employment. What can the widow do! What about the deserted wife? The cry of the widow and orphan, the suffering of the friendless is daily before the eyes of the God England professes to serve.'

Mary in disguise

Chapter 7 London Evidence

Although Mary had concentrated much of her efforts on the plight of homeless girls and women, this did not mean that she was not interested in the problems of male employment and homelessness. Respectable men could lose their jobs and would sometimes find themselves homeless. It was not uncommon to tramp from town to town in search of work. Many had to sleep outside and could finish up in prison. Some tragically died. During the winter of 1903-1904, the time of our tramping, there were about 300 people known to be sleeping out every night in Manchester and the figure for London was much higher. Mary had a great deal of empathy with those who were trying to find work and was appalled by the numbers. Relating them to the real suffering of individuals who could find themselves on the wrong side of the law she wrote,

'The fate of many unfortunates is a career of gradual physical and moral deterioration from which there is, humanely speaking, no escape. A man may begin a prison career accidentally. An incident related to me is as follows: A man went to a place where there was a local merry- making, hoping to pick up a little work. There was no room in either tramp ward or lodging-house; he slept out, unfortunately for him, on private grounds. For this, he got three months' imprisonment.'

Mary had read widely on the subject and gathered evidence from men as well as women. To add to this, she made a visit to a labour colony in Essex set up by General Booth of the Salvation Army. These colonies, Mary told me, were popular in Germany and provided training and work. However, she felt that they were not suitable for the regular worker who had become unemployed. Different solutions were needed for the different types of unemployment.

'The men's needs and provisions should be better correlated and classified,' said Mary, 'for example, those not capable of work would need a permanent home other than the workhouse, where they could remain for life. Our workhouses and Police Courts deal over and over again with the same individual.'

'Yes, but what can be done?' I asked.

'I think that effective training under efficient control at the right age might save him and the community from many evils.' Mary replied.

'What sort of training would be best?'

'At Hadleigh Farm Colony in Essex, men are trained in farming, market gardening, brick making and construction.'

I asked her what could be done for homeless women.

'The requirements of women also needed to be classified, especially as many homeless girls and women resort to prostitution. I think that those who are habitual tramps could go also. I want to see women and children disappear altogether from the roads.'

We both knew that some men were not really capable of earning enough to support themselves. She told me that some writers were using the phrase 'social wreckage.'

'It's a real concern that the numbers of people with low mentality are increasing at a fast rate. Something needs to be done to stop the degeneration of our race.' said Mary.

'Yes, many of those who can't even provide for themselves do seem to be having a lot of children.' I ventured.

'It seems only right that society should put restriction of the multiplication of those who are economically useless.'

'How can that be done?'

'Sterilization. The mere stoppage of the breeding of mentally deficient children would, in the end, be a gain the state.'

Mary was not alone in advocating sterilization. Other supporters of what was termed Eugenics were H.G. Wells and George Bernard Shaw.

In 1904 Mary published her views on *How to Deal with the Unemployed.* This book gained her a prize and national recognition from the Religious Society of Friends (The Quakers), an organization with which she was to have much greater contact in future years. The purpose of Mary's undercover investigations, consequent reports, talks and writings was to bring about change. In November 1904 Mary was asked to appear as a witness before the Local Government Board Departmental Committee of Enquiry into Vagrancy. This was an opportunity to express her views to those who had the power to make changes. A group of government officials, led by Sir William

Chance, interviewed her at length. She was asked why she felt it necessary to visit the places.

'I became convinced that there was some cause driving women down into destitution, and I was surprised that when you asked women to go to the vagrant ward they considered it was no refuge for them. I wondered why this was, and what the nature was of the provision that our country made; and therefore I determined to investigate it.'

Mary was eager to relate her first-hand experiences to the men and to express her views on how conditions could be improved. She began by giving them an abridged version of our treatment at the casual ward of North Brierley workhouse. After she had described the way in which we were sexually intimidated by the pauper who was in sole charge of taking our details in lodge, she was asked, 'Why did you not write directly to the Board of Guardians of the workhouse?'

The names of the different establishments were now known but Mary wanted to explain why she had initially felt it prudent not to name the establishments and to use a pseudonym in her reports. As an undercover investigator, she was worried about the legal consequences of her actions and revelations. She replied, 'In fact, I may say I was at first afraid of being put in prison for having gone. I quite thought they had legal power over me to put me in prison; therefore I was naturally very chary about making my experience public.'

Another member of the committee asked what other things personally upset her about the conditions she found. One of the real horrors for her was the presence of bugs and vermin, particularly finding them in her bed. She passionately told the officials of her reaction to them, 'I had never seen the animals in my life before I went into those places; it was a terrible thing for me.'

She went on to say how very difficult it was to eat food without a drink. She stressed that a drink was necessary after hours of hard physical work, which caused perspiration and therefore loss of fluid. It was wrong to not be given the means to quench her thirst.

'Mrs. Higgs, I am wondering why you did not simply ask for water?'

Asking for something, as Oliver Twist had done, would be viewed as impertinent and could probably result in even harsher treatment. The interviewers were privileged men and Mary knew that they would find it extremely difficult to understand how intimidated a poor vulnerable woman would feel in the circumstances. In her reply Mary tried to convey how helpless she felt in her guise of a tramp, when confronted by those with power over her,

'I do not think you can quite form a sort of conception of the terror that comes over you from workhouse officials. This official was remarkably sharp; she hardly allowed us time to get in and out of the bath. She ordered us about as if we were slaves; we scarcely dared speak to her; she seemed as if she would snap you up for anything; we were perfectly frightened of her.'

Of course, she was right in thinking that it was very unlikely that they could form any sort of idea. They would never find themselves in such a vulnerable position!

Mary gave evidence of her treatment at the casual ward in Manchester, describing how hard she had worked on very little food and how both she and I had become ill as a result.

The work had included spending two hours unravelling oakum followed by cleaning three lounges and two WCs, then scrubbing all the way down a staircase while workmen walked up and down it. All this before noon! The government official suggested that she found the work hard because of her general comfort at home.

'The women who use the tramp wards are well accustomed to this type of work and therefore they would not find it too arduous. You are not used to this sort of physical work. Therefore I put it to you that this is why it seemed so taxing.'

By then Mary must have felt exasperated. Her indignant reply was, 'I am a minister's wife on a poor salary, and I have been accustomed to working hard all my life; therefore I do not think I suffered as much as some of these poor women.'

Speaking about me, Mary proudly said that I was a working woman who could do any work, for example doing the washing for seven people.

Eventually they asked for her recommendations with regard to women vagrants. Mary said that she wanted to see women and children disappear altogether from the roads. She thought that married women who were tramping with their husbands should be taken into the workhouse proper and their husbands made to pay. They should be allowed to go out again with their husbands if it was thought that the man was travelling for work. Children would also be much better off in the workhouse than in the casual ward.

'I propose that single women should be received into the workhouse proper. I would do away with the casual ward for women. The reason of that would be three-fold. First of all, the woman, if she was admitted into the workhouse proper, would be given workhouse clothes; therefore her own would not be destroyed. She would go out in as good a state of cleanliness as before. Besides that, I think it is altogether wrong to recognize a class of vagrant women at all. I think it is a great evil to recognize that a woman has the right to go about from place to place in that unattached kind of way. I think she should be received at the workhouse proper. I think it is a mistake for our country to educate any woman into vagrancy.'

When asked for her recommendations on the food, she was particularly keen to make sure that adequate liquid was provided at each meal, suggesting tea, coffee, cocoa or hot water be provided to make their own tea. The lack of drink was something which she had found particularly irksome. She also advised that gruel should only be served for one meal and that bread and cheese be given at midday. In addition, she proposed the appointment of a Lady Protector at every Workhouse who would interview each woman and record the information on a form. Mary proudly told the committee that she had done this role in Oldham for five years and gave them a copy of the form she had produced herself, adding that she copied them at her own expense.

Mary also held strong convictions on the way homeless men should be treated, firmly disagreeing with the two-day detention rule, except in the case of hardened vagrants, arguing that men should be discharged early to look for work. She expressed her views on those who were not capable of being self-supporting, referred to in those days as 'feeble minded', suggesting that they could be prevented from 'drifting about' by some form of compulsory detention.

After the interview, the committee produced a report, which took Mary's views very seriously. It was in complete agreement with her on the view that women should not be admitted to casual wards.

'We feel that a great advantage would ensue from the closing of the casual wards to women in this country.'

They also said that the accusations made by Mary, whose evidence was based in first-hand experience, could not be ignored.

Up to this time, Mary had no personal experience of the conditions for the homeless in the capital. She had been told that, if anything, they were worse than in the north. So far she had been deterred from sampling them because she feared that she would not be in a fit state to be received into the house of her respectable friends. However she decided it would be a good idea to take a look at the common lodging houses available when she was asked to give a talk in London in early 1905. I was not able to go with her, so she persuaded her son Arthur to accompany her on the venture. Again, she adopted the disguise of a woman of the vagrant class. Arthur, an electrical engineer in his early 20s, was dressed as a poor working man. His main role was to shadow his mother. Starting near one of the main train stations, probably Euston, Mary asked an old woman selling apples where she might find a bed for the night. The woman told her about two places, but advised against the first, 'If you are respectable,' she said. The other accommodation was what the apple woman described as a charity place. Mary decided to look at both places. It proved to be difficult to find the first one, and as they got near Mary noticed that there were doubtful characters hanging around. A woman who lived on the street advised Mary against going to the lodging house, so this time she took the advice. She then made her way to the charity house, but the cost was eight pennies per night, hardly charity. It was above what she wanted to pay as an investigator.

Mary wondered if there was a tramp ward where a woman with no money might stay. She walked down a busy street with booths and market stalls along the sides. Mary approached a woman selling candles and asked, 'Can you tell me where the spital is?'

The woman, who knew that Mary meant the tramp ward of the workhouse, looked at Mary piteously. 'You poor thing.' the woman said, 'Have you got to go there?'

As she got near, Mary asked again about the tramp ward and was again spoken to with pity. She decided not to stay, but vowed that she would return. When I accompanied her at later date, we realised that the woman's pity was justified.

As she could not find out about any other lodgings nearby and had already spent about an hour looking, Mary rejoined her son. Then they did something that real tramps would never do because of the cost. They took a bus to central London. After getting directions from a policeman, they came to a lodging house for men with one for women next door. I don't know the precise location, but Mary told me that place was situated up a narrow entry from one of London's well-known thoroughfares.

As there were separate facilities for women, Arthur was not needed, so he went for a walk around the area while his mother went inside. Mary found that she had to go through the men's lodging house and pay a man who was playing cards before she would be allowed in. The other card players looked at Mary but did not speak. She paid and was directed through to the women's part. Upstairs a group of women in hats sat around. Others came in and out but Mary, as a stranger, did not feel welcome. The woman who appeared to be in charge directed Mary downstairs. She found herself in a long cellar. The room was damp and dingy as the only light came from a window, which was partly below ground. This was the only downstairs room and was used as a sitting room and kitchen. There was a fireplace and a hob but no oven. Some women were sitting on wooden benches beside tables. Even in the dim light, Mary could see heaps of dirt and bits of food under the tables. The cost was six pennies, compared with four pennies in the north, but the cooking facilities were even worse. Mary spoke to a woman who looked like a hawker.

'Is six pence what you would expect to pay in London?' she asked.

'You'd be lucky to get anything cheaper. This one took a good bit of getting.' replied the woman.

The deputy came in carrying a large bunch of keys, 'Anyone for bed?' she shouted. Mary made an excuse and left.

When she had rejoined Arthur it was decided that it would be a good idea for him to visit the men's part of the house. She could not get first-hand experience of the conditions of the men's part, but she would be able to add Arthur's findings to her report. His account proved that the conditions were even worse. He entered the grimy common sitting room. Like the women's it was a half cellar so there was very little natural light. Men were sitting around smoking and spitting bits of tobacco onto the dirty concrete floor. Arthur could see that dust and the debris of meals had simply been swept under the wooden table which stood in the centre of the room. The lodging house owner then showed Arthur to the bedroom. Arthur looked around the room. A notice on the wall stated that;

GENTLEMEN ARE REQUESTED NOT TO GO TO BED IN THEIR BOOTS

When Arthur checked the blankets, it was clear that no notice had been taken of the sign, because the blankets were filthy. Arthur was not surprised that the men would choose to sleep in their boots. A pair of boots was a prize possession, and it was feared that they would be stolen during the night if they were removed.

Although neither of them spent the night at the lodging houses, Mary felt that the exercise was worthwhile when she came to give her talk. However, she decided that on a future visit to London, it would be useful to stay in a casual ward to gather more information.

Mary was willing to put up with a great deal of indignity, discomfort and even sickness in order to gather the evidence she felt was necessary to put before the authorities and those whom she thought could bring about change. So, when Mary was asked to give another talk in London she invited me to accompany her. By this time, Mary had given many talks, published reports and given evidence to the authorities, so had become well known to those involved in the running of workhouses. Apart from the time she went to London with Arthur, her reports referred to herself and an anonymous female companion. Mary thought that if we went together she might be recognised and that would make the investigation invalid.

One day in March 1905, we donned our disguise and caught the train to London. It was a pleasant evening, around 6 pm, when we arrived at the casual ward of a workhouse. This particular place had been chosen by Mary because, according to the Workhouse Guardians, it was well-regulated, clean and boasted real beds and porcelain baths. We entered separately and found there was only one other woman, who was due to leave the following morning. The place looked spotlessly clean due no doubt to the hard work of the inmates. We were given brown bread and gruel, but the bread was sour. After a hot bath the woman in charge gave us clean nightclothes, led us to our cells, and locked the doors at 7 pm. Although we had real beds, the cells were like those used to house prisoners. I settled down, but soon heard Mary vomiting violently in the cell next door. I soon began coughing and feeling ill. In the cell at my other side was the other woman, Sarah, who was coughing and retching. It was dark, there was no water and no means to summon help. In the morning we got up at 5.30 am. Mary asked Sarah if she had seen a doctor as her cough sounded like asthma or even bronchitis. Sarah said that she would try to get into the infirmary when she left. None of us was able to eat the salty gruel which was served in an old enamel mug. Sarah pointed to a thick layer of scrum on the top of the gruel. She had been detained in the ward for three days because she had stayed in another casual ward during the month. Sarah told us that she had what she referred to as 'business' in that part of the city and often had to stay in the tramp wards.

At 7 am we were put under the charge of an old woman and set to work. Mary was told to clean four cells and the long passage which led past nine cells on one side and the same number on the other. After that she had two bathrooms and a lavatory with two water closets to clean. She was provided with a bucket, cloth and washing soda but no apron.

The old woman proved to be an exacting taskmaster. I was given similar work; bathrooms, a whole flight of stairs and even a private sitting room, which was usually done by the matron. Everything had to be done in a particular way, even down to the folding of blankets which had to be made into an exact shape. A high standard was expected even though it was known that we had not been able to eat. Mary found no sympathy from the matron who knew she had been very sick and had not eaten. In fact it appeared that the matron and her deputy thought that sickness was some sort of dodge. I worked hard but when Mary set about the tasks given her, she proved to be less diligent and feeling unwell, did less work when she thought she was not being watched. Not knowing we were friends, the matron spoke disparagingly of Mary, 'I can't abide that old tramp. She's been eating stale fish. That's what made her sick. I can always tell that sort. I always know what people are like.'

I knew this would amuse Mary, so managed to tell her while we were changing the water in our buckets. She found it so humorous that she said it relieved the situation and confessed that she was guilty of a bit of 'scamping' when she thought the matron was not watching her.

After five solid hours we had a break for food. I managed to eat a little bread and cheese, but Mary was still unable to eat. She looked wretched as she laid her head on the table. The matron looked at the uneaten food as if it were an expensive delicacy and said, 'What a pity.'

I believe she thought the pity was the waste of food, not Mary's sickness which prevented her from eating.

There then followed another four hours of cleaning. Mary was given five very ornate forms to clean, followed by two long tables. The wood had to be scrubbed white with soap and water. Then she had to kneel to scrub the floor and the underside of the forms. She looked quite faint. I could see that the deputy was not pleased with her work and was finding it hard to keep her temper. Meanwhile I worked as hard as possible in the circumstances and finished cleaning two bedrooms. I was so tired that I hoped to have a short rest but I was then told to clean the storeroom. The deputy recognised my hard work and brought me two slices of bread and butter and a cup of tea. While the deputy was watching someone else, I managed give Mary a drink of the tea, but it was a mistake because it made her violently sick.

At last, we were allowed to stop at 5 pm. It is impossible to describe how tired we felt having worked on so little food, but still neither of us felt we could touch the meal given to us. Mary's sickness was ignored, but I was given a lozenge to ease my sore throat. At 5.30 pm we went to bed. I felt cold and my limbs ached. Mary, in the next cell was unable to sleep because of her sickness. These were her thoughts,

'The cross-bars of the window faintly seen against the sky spoke of the cross that is never absent, of the woes of men and of Him who is crucified in the least of these, His brethren. When will the long torture of the ages be gone, and men care for the poor?'

Even though I was desperately tired, I did not sleep well. At 6.30 am we were allowed to get up and rinse our mouths with water. How my body ached. Despite being in good health before the investigation, Mary was particularly badly affected. Not long after we left she started to haemorrhage, a problem she told me she had experienced in the past. She believed that the severity of the treatment in the tramp ward had caused it. Mary had to remain in London for medical treatment. She was fortunate to be able to stay with her eldest daughter Mary, for it was a month before she regained her strength. She reflected on how the treatment might affect those who were much more vulnerable than she was.

Chapter 8 Lodging with Prostitutes

We were looking forward to the Beautiful Oldham Society's spring flower show of 1905. The Society had continued to develop, or should that be grow, and had the support of influential men and women in the town. For example, Winston Churchill one of the town's MPs, was an Officer for the years 1904 and 1905.

The spring flower shows were held at Werneth Park. In preparation, bulbs and compost had been sold in schools at cost in the previous autumn. Children were encouraged to plant the bulbs, keep them in a dark place and then nurture them for the display at the show. Artistic ability was also encouraged and careful observational drawings or paintings of plants were executed. All this was very popular with children who did not have gardens and saw so little greenery in the town. It also encouraged healthy competition.

It was the spring of 1905 and the committee was busy setting up for the big day. Mrs. and Miss Lees were happy to use their glasshouse at Werneth Park for the occasion. Tables were set up for the exhibits and everything was made ready. By this time the Junior Society had an amazing 6,000 young members. That year 66 exhibits out of a total of 192 were by elementary school children. It was a delight to see the lovely display of colourful plants and pictures.

'Isn't it just wonderful?' exclaimed the ever-enthusiastic Mary.

'It all looks so beautiful,' I replied taking in the array of shades and the lovely perfume of some of the plants.

Couples came and admired the exhibits. Children came with their parents, or more often with their teachers and looked wide-eyed at the beautiful arrangement of flowering bulbs. Some were excited to see their plants or artwork on display.

**Ladies of the Beautiful Oldham Society Committee.
Mary is in the centre of the front row.**

Junior members of the Beautiful Oldham Society at Clarksfield School

Those who had won prizes were invited to a special prize giving ceremony. The proud winners were presented with certificates, which were greatly valued.

Many Oldhamers remember these annual shows and competitions with affection. As well as the spring flower shows, there were summer garden and back yard competitions, and autumn allotment shows. The experience was shared with other towns in the National Gardens Guild. Members of the Beautiful Oldham Society gave talks in other areas, for example to the Lincoln Branch of the National Union of Women Workers in October 1905. Over many years, the Beautiful Oldham Society raised awareness of environmental issues. It introduced countless children, who lived in houses without gardens, to the pleasure of planting bulbs and waiting for them to grow and flower into a thing of beauty. A good example of this was the pretty garden planted and tended by staff and children at Clarksfield School.

There was still work to be done to achieve Mary's long term aim of improving conditions for the homeless. One of the reasons for our investigations was to show that prostitutes used the lodging houses. Mary asked me if I would accompany her again. She decided that she wanted to spend three nights in lodging houses to gain a valuable insight into the problems. In May of 1905, we took a train to Huddersfield and then a tram to the area which Mary wanted to visit. We arrived in the early evening at a rather respectable looking house. It was a large tall building, set back from the road, with a small front garden. A couple of young children playing in the hallway called, 'Missus,' to summon assistance. A stout woman waddled towards us. 'Beds are six punce each, but you will have to share a room with strangers,' she said. This was rather more than we had thought, and we had only budgeted for four pennies each per night. Still Mary felt that she needed to gather more evidence to she agreed to let the woman in charge show us into the small, clean kitchen. There were two short benches, a table and a dresser. There was a sink and shelves to hold pots. A door led to a yard with a 'convenience'. There was a good fire and hot water, so we sat to rest and chat with the other women there. The oldest woman was busying herself and appeared to help the woman in charge. There was a middle-aged woman who looked rather genteel but when she spoke with her soft Scottish accent there was a strong smell of liquor on her breath. The only other woman in the room was a young neatly dressed woman whom we later found was called Martha. When we had warmed ourselves, we went to look around the area and to buy a few provisions to bring back. By then it was 10 pm so we decided to go into the common sitting room to see if anyone was there. Most of the women in the room were young and preparing to go out. We watched in amazement as they quickly transformed themselves ready to go out on the streets: hair was curled, cheeks reddened and eyebrows blackened. After they had left, we went to the kitchen to prepare a snack. The Scotswoman started boasting that she had been drunk every day that week. She soon left the house, probably in search of more drink. We settled down with our cups of tea, buttered bread, and listened to Martha's story. She had met and fallen in love with a sailor who had asked her to marry him. Her mother, a widow, did not approve of the match, but Martha had gone against her mother's wishes and married. The couple had moved to Huddersfield to live with his parents, but they found this very difficult because his mother did not take to Martha. After an argument, Martha's husband told her he was going back to sea and not coming back. She would have to fend for herself. It was impossible to stay with his parents because they knew she had been deserted. She had tried to get work in service but even though she was only 22, found that they preferred younger unmarried girls. She was using what money she had saved to pay for her bed and a little food and hoped to find work soon.

The door opened and a weary looking young woman came in.

'How did you get on?' Asked Martha.

Sally coughed, 'Oh, Martha love, I've been out for more than two hours and not got any money.'

We learned something of how Sally came to be at this place. She had been in service and had stayed out late having been persuaded by a friend to go to a fair in a nearby town. She knew that she had stayed out longer than she should and as her employer was strict, she was afraid to return. Her companion said, 'Don't go back, Sally, Misses'll only scold you. Let's stay in a lodging house for the night.'

'It had seemed like a good idea especially as I had been treated to a small drink at the fair. But in the morning I realised that I had very little money and no job to go to. A girl who was staying there told me she had been out the night before and earned money. I was urged to go with her the next night.'

Mary and I now fully understood the character of the house. We went up to our bedroom at midnight. The room had seven low, iron bedsteads with reasonably clean wire mattresses, sheets and pillows.

Many of the girls did not come came back until about 2 am. Several were drunk and singing bawdy songs.

After a restless night, we were woken by the proprietress. We brewed some tea and borrowed a knife to butter our bread. Sally was coughing, but we noticed that she was not eating.

'Have a little bread and butter,' Mary offered.

Sally gratefully accepted this and a cup of sweet tea. She told us that she had no family or friends to help her, and had been starved into prostitution. As we ate, women came in to cook their breakfasts, and the smell of bacon, onions and beefsteak gradually filled the room. A small group was sitting around the fire, smoking, drinking, and singing music hall songs. A couple of girls were dancing to the tune. Suddenly one shrieked, and moved quickly to one side, as she saw three huge blackjacks (big beetles) moving in the corner. Skirts were quickly pulled up to prevent the black shiny creatures from crawling up them, and benches were moved to the centre of the room before the company could settle. Just then, a young woman came in crying bitterly.

'What's t' do Lily?' Sally asked.

'A've bin to t'doctors,' she sniffed, 'E's sending mi t'lock ward.'

There were sympathetic comments and assurance of the merits of lock wards for the treatment of venereal disease, always a risk for prostitutes.

'Never mind, Lily, you'll soon be through with it,' said the Scotswoman.

As we were reflecting on the fate of the young woman, a distressed mother came in looking for her daughter. She told how the daughter had been wrongly accused of stealing. The mother had traced her to another lodging house, but she had left. My throat tightened as she said,

'Whatever she's done, I'll see her through it and take her home, If only I can find her. She's my best friend.'

Looking around at the girls in the room, she added, 'If you come across her, tell her that the back door is always open, and she'll be welcome.'

On hearing this several girls started to cry, no doubt thinking of their own mothers. The scene brought tears to our eyes and those of our young friend, Martha.

'That's what your mother will say,' Mary told her kindly.

Martha offered to take the distraught mother to another lodging house to look for her daughter.

Mary and I were glad of the opportunity to learn more about the lives of the women who came to stay in the place. We heard stories of theft, cheating and ill-treatment. It was not difficult to see how a girl could finish up there. Dolly told us how she had taken to a hotel for the night by a man who looked like a 'toff'. When she awoke, he had gone without giving her any money.

Eliza, a servant had been seduced by her employer but when he found she was pregnant, she was dismissed. She would soon have to go to the workhouse to have the baby, but did not know how she would then manage.

Another girl complained that she had been given copper coins, silvered over. 'Now, I always examine the coins, scrape them with my nails, and bite them, anything to make sure they're what they should be.' she explained.

Mary believed them when they told her they would like a different life, but could not find a way out. Although she could not directly help, as that would ruin our 'incognito', she managed to pass addresses of those who could, to the girls she felt would benefit.

The following morning we left and took a penny tram ride to the town centre. We went to look at a couple of lodging houses we had been told of, but decided they were too small. Mary wanted to see as much 'life' as possible and gather plenty of evidence, so we made our way to a larger one which was situated on a main road. The sizeable houses must have once been occupied by the better-off but had now degenerated into profit-making lodging houses. The lodging house for women stood next to the one for men. The door stood open so we walked along a passage, which led to the kitchen. At one side of the welcoming fire was a hot water boiler and at the other side, a small sink. There were two tables and two forms, which could seat about four people each. On the wall were shelves for clothes and hats, and another for a few pots and two large tins. These were multi-purpose – we saw them full of dirty pots, clothes being washed in them, and feet being soaked in them. When we heard that one of the girls had a contagious disease, but had refused to go to the hospital, we decided not to eat or drink there.

A young woman was getting ready to go out for the night. We were shocked to see that she sat in full view of the open front door, dressed only in a good quality, but dirty, chemise and underskirt. She put powder on her face and breast and rouge on her cheeks, then burned a match and used it to blacken her eyebrows. Next, she rolled her hair into curls and put a net over it to keep it in place. Then she put on a very thin muslin blouse, a costume skirt and a jacket, which was open at the neck. Finally, she chose a hat to complete the outfit. There were a number to choose from, because although they had owners, hats were regarded as common property. Mary was concerned about the health as well as the moral vulnerability of the thin, pale woman. She had a severe cough and could hardly speak when she went out for the night with very little to cover her chest. Mary did not think that she would live long, especially when she was told that a girl had died at the house the previous week.

We soon fell into conversation with some of the women in the house. Clara, a young widow with a baby, had been going around to people she knew, begging a penny or halfpenny from each to pay for her bed. The little boy was well nourished and contented and his mother was proud of his chubby legs. She told Mary that she sometimes had to spend the night outside with the baby if she could not beg money for the night.

Elsie said that she had managed to do a day charring which had been hard work but well paid. She showed generosity to those less fortunate, sharing the food she had been able to buy. Several only had the money for the lodgings, which left them with nothing for food.

When Mary wrote about our experience, she was determined to give her readers an insight into of the lives of some of the unfortunate women she encountered. Showing her empathy with the plight of the young prostitutes, Mary took the opportunity to criticize the system and to suggest an alternative:

'I have before had occasion to notice the harm done by hospital authorities in sending friendless girls, without sufficient enquiry (or even though knowing they are quite friendless), back to their native town. Girls such as this should be passed on to some agency that would 'mother' them. It is easy to see how a little indecision, and the pressure of hunger, might anchor a girl to sin. For most of those who

entered were openly leading a life of shame. Girl after girl came in, rested, and went out.'

**Beautiful
Oldham Badge**

Chapter 9 Improved Accommodation

Mary's reports were starting to have the desired effect. In October 1905, she was asked to speak at a conference held by the Women Guardians and the Local Government Association at Manchester town hall to discuss the need for women's lodging houses in the city. Miss Margaret Ashton, the honorary secretary spoke,

'The conditions that the poor homeless women have to endure were brought to the attention of this Association when we were asked to publish a very terrible pamphlet.'

She now had the full attention of the room.

'The pamphlet was Five Days and Nights as a Tramp by Mary Higgs. The revelations were so startling and appalling that the Association has since conducted an investigation to see what accommodation there was in the large towns for women who, whilst of the poorest class, were still striving to earn a decent living.'

The listeners waited.

'The Common Lodging Houses are sinks of iniquity, and their sanitary conditions are such that they could not be described at a public meeting.'

A councillor reported that there was only one municipal lodging house in Lancashire and that was in Darwen, and gave examples of municipal lodging houses for both men and women in Glasgow. Mary was then asked to speak. She described the Salvation Army Shelters for women in other towns and declared that while she was fully in favour of a Municipal Lodging House for Manchester, she suggested that a Salvation Army Shelter might be needed as well. The Lord Mayor, Sir Thornhall Shann spoke,

'I am of the opinion that municipal institutions are more expensive to run than private ones. It would be better for the Corporation, if it

were to take any action, to build a house and then let the Salvation Army run it.

We would have to wait and see what the Corporation in Manchester decided to do. Meanwhile the practical reality of helping the homeless in Oldham was tackled head-on by Mary. The rescue home in Esther Street could accommodate three girls or women, four at a pinch. Many of these had babies or young children, and it was clear that more accommodation was desperately needed.

Mary spoke to Sarah Lees about her ideas to secure a larger place. 'We need a house with at least three bedrooms, a parlour, kitchen and scullery,' said Mary.

Sarah was always ready to listen to Mary's ideas. She was generous in her support of schemes to help those who found themselves in unfortunate positions, often through no fault of their own. In 1906, Mrs. Lees purchased Bent House, a Georgian mansion situated near the top of West Street.

Mary and I were impatient to see the house. The road was cobbled and on the pavement in front of the house stood an iron gas lamp. A brick wall had been built to separate the house from the road. Pillars held the wrought iron gate, and matching iron railings ran along the top of the wall. The substantial stone house had an imposing entrance. Classical pillars flanked a solid wooden door with its brass knocker. Above the door was a half circle window with stained and leaded glass. This was capped by a stone triangle, which rested on the pillars. Above this was a sash window, topped with a stone triangle to match the one above the door. There were four tall windows to the left and four to right of the door. At each end of the roof, seven chimney pots stood to attention on two high chimneystacks, proclaiming the importance of the house. In the centre of the roof, another stack held more pots.

The musty smell of a closed up building greeted us as we stepped inside. We were unsure how long it had been empty but the cobwebs and unloved atmosphere had enveloped the bare room. This once imposing house had nineteen rooms including attics. We walked into a large room with a grand fireplace. Mary was already making plans. 'This will be the communal living room.'

There was a roomy kitchen, and beyond an ample scullery.

'The women can use that cupboard for their belongings and have their own keys,' she said pointing to a large cupboard built into the alcove at the side of the large fireplace.

We walked into the scullery. 'The women will be able to do their own washing here. And they should do their own cleaning too.'

Outside in the yard were WCs. Back inside, we walked up the wide staircase to find a bathroom and bedrooms. More bedrooms could be organised in the attic space. The house was ideal for use as a hostel.

'No smoking should be allowed in the bedrooms,' said Mary,

I agreed. Mary thought a little and then added, 'but some old women cannot go without a pipe,' she added, feeling that some leeway should be given when deemed appropriate.

We soon set about getting the place ready to take in homeless women and girls. A carefully selected matron was to be put in charge and Mary, as secretary would be in overall control. It would not be long before the place would be alive with the sound of women and children. Although she was a deeply religious woman, she believed in religious tolerance and stated that it was important not to favour any denomination and that prayers should not be compulsory. She had a view of the matron as a mother figure who would guide the lives of her charges and suggested she lead simple prayers and keep books to lend and even read to the women occasionally in the evening.

'It must be remembered that the approach to poor women must be very simple, and that Christian character and kindly care appeal to them more than services of a formal nature.'

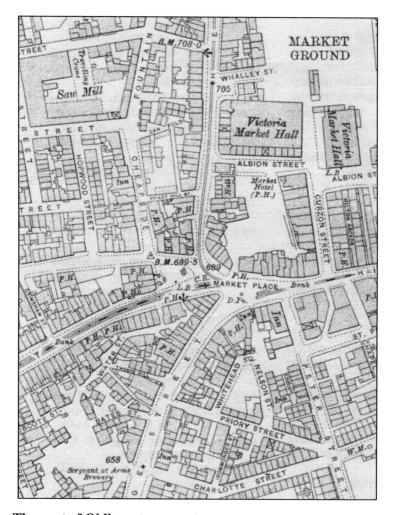

The west of Oldham town centre

Streets from top left: New Radcliffe Street, Boardman Street, Grosvenor Street, West Street, (BM698.5) Manchester Street (with the tramline.)

The housing between Boardman Street and Grosvenor Street and bordered by Hopwood Street to the east and Rochdale Road to the west was particularly overcrowded. West Street is very close to the town centre. At that time the houses in the area were particularly cramped and many were old. In Oldham, the infant mortality rate was almost six times as high as the national average. Towns like ours had grown quickly, packing workers into unhealthy living spaces. The mill owners and others in the growing middle class were able to move into the suburbs, but the majority of people lived in overcrowded, unsanitary conditions, often in back-to-back, hastily built housing. As a result, it could be seen that there was a need to create better housing for everyone. Ebenezer Howard, founder of the Garden City Movement, was well-known to Mary as he had spoken in the town and stayed at Greenacres parsonage. He advocated the building of new towns, not for the profit of the builders, but with the interests of the habitants paramount. The members of the Beautiful Oldham Society were particularly interested in the Hampstead Garden Suburb Trust. Mary wrote to the Oldham Chronicle extolling the idea. This resulted in the formation of the Oldham Garden Suburb Tenants Ltd. in 1906. This was a small enterprise compared to that of a Garden City, but the theory behind the scheme was sound, as can be seen from the prospectus, giving the aims of the association:

'To promote the co-operative owner-ship and administration of an estate which, while avoiding the dangers which frequently accompany speculative building devoid of public spirit, will harmonize the interest of the investor.'

By creating a limited company, the Oldham Garden Suburb Tenants were able to sell shares to raise money. A plot of about fifty acres at Hollins Green was bought from Sarah Lees for £150 per acre, a price 'considerably below its market value'.

The area fitted the criteria because it looked out to open countryside yet was only a short tram ride to the town centre. There were plans for 700 semi-detached houses with gardens. The houses were to be no more than fourteen to an acre. They were to cost £183 each and were to be rented at 5s 9d per week excluding rates. This was an exciting, but long term development.

Meanwhile Bent House at 180 West Street was ready to accommodate homeless girls and women. There was no shortage of those needing beds, but it was proving difficult to find work for the girls and women. Mary understood that without work, the same women would have to return again and again for help. So, once more Mary took the initiative. She became an entrepreneur when she started a paper sorting enterprise at Bent House. This small business generated an income to help the women to be more self-reliant.

Bent House

In addition to the practical work in Oldham, Mary continued to use her pen to bring about change. She had gained quite a national reputation for her views on unemployment and homelessness and was pleased that her work was recognised in academic circles. In 1906, she received the Gamble Prize presented by her old College, Girton, for her essay on *'Vagrancy, its causes, history and treatment in England and in other countries.'*

This piece was later used, along with other material in her book *'Glimpses into the Abyss.'* The reviewer of the Manchester Guardian commented on her orderly and methodical method of research and was particularly impressed by her fortitude in the face of personal hardship. He wrote,

'The value of the investigating work which Mrs. Higgs has set herself to do with such persistence is now generally admitted. The systematic way in which she has tackled agency after agency, district after district deserves all praise, and the more so when one appreciates the degree of personal pain and suffering (even danger) involved in each experiment and the very real courage needed to face them voluntarily time after time.'

The book also received a favourable review in the Economical Journal by William Beveridge who became the Director of Labour Exchanges in 1909. He wrote,

'For the most part, knowledge as to this class has come to us through the various institutions which provide for it, that is to say, from the accounts of those in charge of casual wards, shelters, and common lodging houses. Mrs. Higgs is able to show the homeless life from another point of view, and to supplement the study of the vagrant by knowledge and criticism of the institutions as they appear to the vagrant.'

(NB the Beveridge Report of the 1940s became the basis of the modern Welfare State).

In Manchester, progress had been made in the provision of a municipal lodging house. Mary was pleased to tell me that The Women Guardians and the Women's Local Government Association had sent a deputation to the Sanitary Committee of Manchester

Council, with the result that in March 1907 the city council agreed to build a women's municipal lodging house. Land situated behind Victoria Station was chosen. I felt sure that this would not have been possible without Mary's damning reports which gave the case the urgency that it deserved.

Meanwhile the campaign to allow women more say in the running of the country was gaining pace. Mary felt that not only could women achieve a great deal in society, but that their input was a necessity and said that, 'in every department of national life, fathering needed the supplement of motherhood.'

Chapter 10 Women in Public Life

The early years of the new century were a time of great activity for women's societies. In Oldham, the committee of the National Union of Women Workers, of which Mary was an active member, put a great deal of effort into securing women into positions at local level, with some success. Marjory Lees, secretary of the branch, wrote many letters to Parliament. From 1869 unmarried or widowed women householders and rate payers had been able to vote in local elections. In 1907, members of the Oldham group increased the fight for legislation that would allow women to be elected as members of all local authorities. Meetings, letter writing, protest rallies and the lobbying of MPs were a regular feature of the campaign. That same year, an Act of Parliament allowed women to sit on Town and County Councils and Sarah Lees stood as the Liberal candidate for the Hollywood ward. She won the seat from the Tory and became Oldham's first woman councillor.

Despite this success, progress toward women's suffrage was slow. A group of suffragists, headed by Mrs. Emmeline Pankhurst of Manchester had become increasingly frustrated by the lack of success of the National Union of Women's Suffrage Societies, an association founded in 1897 as an umbrella organisation for the various regional societies. As a result, the Women's Social and Political Union was founded in 1903. When members resorted to militant action they were dubbed the 'suffragettes' by the Daily Mail.

Although Mary fully supported the campaign for women's suffrage, she felt that her main concern was the welfare of society's most vulnerable women and this is where she directed most of her energy.

In the midst of all this activity, Mary experienced a sudden tragedy. In May 1907, her husband Thomas became unwell. After only five days of illness he died of pneumonia at the age of 56. Thomas had given his wife encouragement and support in her many ventures. Mary wrote of his death,

'It was a stunning blow, as all my life had been bound up with his.'

Their lives had been centred around the church in Greenacres and the local community for 16 years. Rev. Thomas Higgs had been a great attribute to the church, leading by example in many social and environmental matters. The church manual (yearly report) recorded,

'His sermons were a notable feature of the pastorate. They bore fruit in missionary effort, in the interest of Church members in social questions, and the place the Church and its minister held in public estimation. He preached his last sermon on 19th May 1907.'

His death meant a radical change to Mary's personal circumstances. Not only did she lose her husband and all that entailed, she also lost her home. It seems ironic that someone who had done so much for homeless women should suddenly find herself a homeless widow at the age of 53. When Mary had to leave the parsonage in Greenacres, her friends Sarah and Marjory Lees helped her to find accommodation. They owned a small property next to Bent House in West Street, known as Bent Cottage. Mary moved in with two of her children. Arthur, who was in 26 and working for Ferranti in Hollinwood, now became the only bread winner. Mabel was 17 and still at school.

West Street was in a very built up area with no views of open countryside, which Mary missed. Without her husband's income it was difficult for her to get away. Fortunately, she had a friend who owned a cottage on the edge of the moors at Heptonstall near Hebden Bridge in West Yorkshire. Mary occasionally rented this to enjoy a break from the town and meet up with her family during holidays.

Mary and her children settled into their new home in the town centre. It must have been difficult for her to adjust but she always had many activities and ventures to occupy her. In 1908, Mary was asked to give evidence before an Inter-departmental Government Committee that had been set up to look into the half-time system in the cotton industry. Mary was to speak as a representative of the Women's Industrial Council, which had been set up in 1894. Male representatives of Trade Unions were also invited to give evidence.

As I had been a half-timer from the age of 11, she asked me and other women at the hostel about the conditions before she attended the meeting.

'The mills are so very hot and dry,' I said.

'What about your clothing?' she asked.

'Being so hot, we wear as little as possible,' replied one woman.
Mary gave a disapproving look. 'Is it very noisy?'
'Oh, it's deafening – clatter, clatter, clatter. Some of the women go
deaf from it, but they soon learn to lip read.'
'Are there many accidents?' Asked Mary.
'Of course, I know a few women who've lost fingers. It's particularly
dangerous for the little ones who have to go under the machines while
they're moving,' I replied.
'Then there's them who get sick, lungs bunged up,' added another
women.
Although children under 14 could not be employed without a
certificate, it was common for 12-year-olds to work half time. At the
meeting with the Government Committee, Mary spoke forcefully
about the educational and physical effect on girls as young as 12
working in factories.

*The conditions are very hot and humid, ripe for disease of all kinds.
The heat induces the young women and girls to wear thin clothing,
which results in a lack of modesty and a temptation to the men in the
mill. Girls under the age of 14 should not be working in mills at all.'*

When asked about the educational effect on half time working she told
them that after six hot and tiring hours in a mill, a girl can hardly be at
her most receptive to learning and many fall asleep. Those who go to
school in the morning fair a little better, but she stressed that the
system stunted any ambition. Unfortunately, school had to be paid for
and many families relied on the small wages that the youngsters could
earn, and saw little advantage in girls continuing their education.
Mary had been very keen for her own three daughters to enjoy the
benefits of higher education, but was very aware that girls were a large
part of the labour force in the cotton towns such as Oldham. Their
income was needed by most local families.
A downturn in the cotton trade that year (1908) meant that employers
wanted to reduce wages by 5%. This was a large amount for workers
to cope with. Therefore, the unions refused and this resulted in the
employers locking the gates of their mills for six weeks. The workers
received a little from the trade unions during the lockout but in most
cases this was not enough. Bent House, being in a central location

and overseen by well-regarded local women, became the administrative centre for the distress fund, which the mayor set up to relieve the ensuing poverty.

Bent House also continued to accommodate homeless women. Mary believed that it would be beneficial to have a countrywide network of suitable places. Consequently, she was the co-founder of the National Association for Women's Lodging-Homes. The president of the council was Her Grace the Duchess of Marlborough and Mary was the Honorary Northern Secretary. Its aims were to link together organisations, to disseminate information and to promote better legislation.

As we have seen, women were finding their way into many areas of public life, but there was still a great deal of inequality in education, work and political involvement. In June 1909 Toronto hosted the International Congress of Women. Delegates from the USA, Europe and Australia attended. Mary travelled to Canada as a representative of the National Council of Women.

Back in Oldham, one of the initiatives in which Mary was involved was coming to fruition. On Saturday 7th August 1909, crowds of people in their Sunday best clothes gathered to mark the occasion of the official opening of the Garden Suburb. We were fortunate to have a lovely sunny day. Work began on the building in March 1908 and by October some families were able to move in. This was an ambitious enterprise which would take time to complete, so it was decided that an official opening ceremony should take place the following year when there were about 150 residents. Ladies carried parasols, gentlemen wore straw hats, girls bonnets and boys caps to keep the sun off their heads. A stage was set up for the speakers. Sarah Lees wore a splendid hat and held a parasol to shade her face. Alfred Emmott wore a top hat and looked very dignified. Ebenezer Howard stood and addressed the audience telling them how impressed he was with the work that had been done so far. He looked very distinguished with his grey hair, bushy, almost white moustache and compassionate eyes. His speech was intended to praise and inspire. He believed that Oldham could be transformed into, *'a town of beautiful and peaceful homes and dwelling places, a place which they would find refreshing to come to from the outside world, a place of intimate associations of sound friendships and good memories.'*

Ebenezer Howard addresses the crowd at the official opening of Garden Suburb, 1909

Ebenezer Howard was rewarded with loud applause from the audience. I did not listen to any more speeches. I wanted to look around and to meet up with Mary and her family. Many of the roads were not finished and some of the land was muddy. I had taken my nephew and found him playing with other boys, pushing sticks and throwing stones into water holes. They had muddy boots, socks and breeches by this time, and would be getting a telling off from their mothers. On the grass a number of working men lounged, some had even taken off their jackets to feel the warmth of the sun through their shirts. A Union Flag was blowing proudly in the breeze. I told my nephew that the band was about to strike up and we went to listen to the Oldham Rifles play marching tunes which we both enjoyed. I then caught sight of Mary and her family and together we watched a display put on by local school children. I was eager to inspect the houses that had been furnished in Green Lane.

Newly built houses in Garden Suburb

The house I looked in was wonderful – a front garden, three bedrooms, a kitchen with a range, a bath, and hot and cold water was laid on. A photographer from the local newspaper wanted to take a photo of Mary ceremoniously planting a tree. She had been the initiator of the idea and was regarded by the newspaper editor as a well-respected citizen. We said goodbye while she went along with a small group to the area that had been chosen for the planting. Marjory Lees, whose family money made the enterprise possible, was also asked to pose for a photograph.

Mary had a life-long interest in child development and education. She believed that education should be for life and that it should involve: a love of nature, a development of self-respect, an understanding of the functions of the body, and an interest in the environment and the wider world. To this end, she began writing weekly articles for the *Oldham Chronicle* and I think, the *Oldham Standard*. The articles took the form of a letter addressed to *My dear young Oldhamer* under the pseudonym *Mrs. Minerva*. Writing with empathy and humour, she desired that the young people have 'clean hearts, big souls, and willing hands!' Moreover, she wanted to make them 'courageous in causes to lift up humanity.' Some of the titles will illustrate the range of subjects: *Clear Skies and Clouds, The Humour of the Situation, Currency Problems, North and South, Dreams, Policewomen, Not by bread alone, Mind, Soul and Spirit.* In the same vein, Mary collaborated with Edward Hayward to produce a pamphlet for the Froebel Society (also known as The Froebel Society for the Promotion of the Kindergarten System) about the development of morality in the child, entitled, *The Evolution of the Child Mind* published in 1910. A practical application of this in Oldham was the establishment at Bent House of a School for Mothers. This in turn, later led to the formation of Municipal Child Welfare Centres in other areas of the town, where help and advice were given to new mothers. With the high infant mortality rate in the town, this was an important initiative. A yearly Baby Show was held in the Music Room of Werneth Park. Here mothers could proudly show off their healthy babies.

A Baby Show in Oldham

Mary also collaborated with Dr. Paton of Nottingham and his son, Lewis, High Master of Manchester Grammar School, to set up the first summer school for the study of social subjects. Here they discussed the child in relation to the family and the community, and topics such as The Report on the Poor Law Commission, and The Land Question were debated. From this grew the Student Christian Movement, (the Copec Movement) an organization that met with experts to discuss social problems from a Christian perspective, but without political bias.

On the 2nd September 1910, the first municipal lodging house in Manchester officially opened. It was named Ashton House in honour of the Manchester councillor and reformer Margaret Ashton.

That year (1910) Mary published what I would call a 'letter to God' under the title *New Creation*. Times must have been difficult for the Higgs family when Thomas was ill and the children were young. Mary's words appear to refer to that time, as she describes her trials and frustrations of married life and motherhood. Even though she uses the word *'joy'*, she sounds disappointed that she had thought marriage to be *'twin companionship'* but found that she had to surrender to a *'patient life of service'*. Despite being a single woman, I was used to the mill girls talking openly about sex, but I was surprised to read Mary's words on the subject. I had thought that women of her class did not discuss the matter, but it is clear that she felt the need to write about it. Here are some of her thoughts, which, in spite of the poetic language, give a clear image of her strong feelings as she complains that her husband only half understands and half pities the pain she suffers.

'Therefore Thou, my Father, gavest me slow toiling years of patient motherhood, the joy of suckling babes, echo of joy born in Thy heart itself, yet pain as well. Is this Thy loving will, my Father God? I thought in airy flights of fancy, union was joy. I find in union pang, yea, anguish born of joy, did I not love, pain were not, but I love, pain seizes me, long days of pain borne patiently as may be, while my other half, half understands, half pities, yet demands a constant sacrifice of life to life. Can love be always joy? The burden grows and life becomes a looking forth to pain. Yet also joy! Joy in conception, joy begot of pain, new birth of love, new life within the soul, joy in surrender of the fancied life of twin companionship for patient life of service, joy in ministry to the imperfect life, the joy of motherhood, what holier joy!

I presume she did not wish to publish the book while her husband was alive, but must have decided that she now wanted to make her thoughts known.

Over the years, Bent House expanded as a social centre and meeting place. The Beautiful Oldham Society continued to meet there and groups such as the Boy Scouts, Girl Guides, a Poetry Society, Mothers' Meeting, and the Workers' Education Association also used the premises. Part of the building continued to be used as a hostel and I became the superintendent. By this time, more women wanted to stay than we could accommodate and the only other provision was the workhouse or the unregulated, run for profit, common lodging houses. Well-regulated places were vital. Fortunately it was decided that another house at 273 West Street would be leased. Hope House, as it was known, was registered as a common lodging-house and was mainly used by servants and those employed in some sort of industry, such as the cotton mills. Some women only stayed there for a night or two, but many returned again and again. Mary, as secretary for both hostels, was kept very busy. She collected and recorded details and wrote a report from the period 1908-1909. Such was the need that at Bent House 6,205 beds were provided in the year and at Hope House 4,600. In addition, 34 destitute women were given free lodgings for short periods. There can be little doubt that many were saved from the workhouse or much worse, by this facility.

In a built up area like West Street, there was very little space for children to play safely. In 1910 Marjory Lees generously gave some land near Bent House to be used as a playground.

By this time, Sarah Lees was a Liberal councillor and women who were the head of a household, were eligible to vote in local elections. However, even after years of campaigning, no women were allowed to vote in national elections. Mary was keen to support the campaign and joined Sarah, Marjory and other like-minded women in founding the Oldham Women's Suffrage Society, a non-militant, non-party organisation. The road to women's suffrage was a long one; however, something momentous for women's equality in Oldham happened that same year. I am proud to state that Sarah Lees was elected as the town's first lady mayor and given the freedom of the town. That made her only the second female mayor in the country, the first being Elizabeth Garrett Anderson, who was elected mayor of Aldeburgh, Suffolk in 1908. During the general election of 1910, Sarah Lees, although she did not have a vote, was the returning officer. I thought it would not be long before women with property, like Sarah Lees, would have the vote. A year later there was a by-election. During the run up Suffragettes set fire to post boxes and broke windows of the Reform Club on Union Street. As a result, women were not allowed into the polling booths. This caused an anomaly. One bobby with a sense of humour asked what he was to do when Sarah Lees visited the polling station: allow her to enter as mayor or prevent her as a woman?

Suffragettes, such as local woman Annie Kenney, gained national publicly for the cause but the main thrust of the campaign in the town was organised by the non-militant Oldham Women's Suffrage Society. This group opened a propaganda shop in Yorkshire Street in the town centre.

Annie Kenny

Sarah Lees

Oldham Reform Club, Union Street

During the following year a large number of Oldham women walked through the streets of Oldham to protest against their inability to vote. All wore their best clothes and followed the banner of the Oldham Suffrage Society.
At a time when Mary was throwing herself into the social needs of the town and beyond, she suffered another serious illness. I do not know what is was, but I feel sure it was due in some part to exhaustion. The doctor told her that she needed to get away to rest and recuperate. She went to stay at the cottage of a friend in Heptonstall, West Yorkshire. She did not want to lose touch with the local work done, so needed the help of a secretary. Miss Martland, who was later to become a public figure in the town, wrote Mary's *Young Oldham* article for the local newspapers. Mary, always ready to help others, found that she had friends who would help her in time of need. Fortunately, she soon regained her strength because 1912 was to prove a memorable year for Mary. Two of her children, Arthur and Mabel married. Arthur married Alice Dunkerley at St. John's church, in Oldham. Alice, affectionately known as Lallie, was an elementary (primary) school teacher. After the marriage Alice joined Mary and Arthur at Bent Cottage.

Mary's youngest daughter Mabel, a talented artist who had attended
Art College, married Herbert T Shawcross. The Quaker ceremony
took place in the town of Ulverston in the Lake District. Mr.
Shawcross came from a wealthy family and was quite a bit older than
Mabel

Suffrage march in Oldham, 1912

.
That same year, a man who had been a friend and inspiration to Mary
died in dramatic circumstances. William T. Stead was sailing to the
USA to give a peace talk when his ship, the Titanic, hit an iceberg.
Stead was among the many that lost their lives. A floral tribute was
sent by Mary, from the 40,000 members of the Lancashire and
Cheshire branch of the Christian Endeavour and the International
Brotherhood.

A Souvenir card to commemorate the visit of the King and Queen to Platt Brothers of Featherstall Road, Oldham

On 12 July 1913 there was great excitement in Oldham as we prepared for a royal visit. People lined the streets to see King George V, Queen Mary and their son, Prince Albert. They made a visit to Platt Brothers, a large manufacturer of textile machinery on Featherstall Road. When Mary learned of the planned visit to the town, she wrote to the palace with details of our work at Bent House. To my surprise and delight, the Queen promised to come to Bent House on her visit to Oldham. The women were very excited when they heard the news. When the day came, we had all made an effort with a little bunting. It was wonderful to have something like this to cheer us. Her Majesty arrived with her ladies in waiting. Although she carried a cane, she walked with stately poise. On her head sat a splendid high brimmed hat with lots of flowers on the crown. Her handsome pale blue costume had a long-line fitted jacket with covered button down the side of the jacket, on the cuffs of the sleeves and down the long skirt.

Under this, she wore a high-necked blouse with a brooch at the neck and earrings. Mary introduced me as the superintendent of the hostel. I felt tongue-tied. The voice that spoke to her did not seem to belong to me. Queen Mary said a few words to the women and sat down for a short time. Mary was the sort of person who could speak to beggars and queens. She never seemed to be at a loss for words and told the Queen all about the scheme. All too soon, it was time for the Queen to go. When she left, one of the mothers sat her small child on the seat vacated by the Queen, and we all laughed with delight at our little 'Royalty'.

In contrast, a group of Oldham women set off on a pilgrimage to the capital later that month. A large contingent of the Oldham Women's Suffrage Society made their way to a national rally in Hyde Park.

By 1913, there were 857 members of the Oldham branch, compared to just 130 in 1911. The rally was attended by 50,000 members of the National Union of Women's Suffrage. After much concerted campaigning, both the Liberal and Labour parties pledged to support votes for women in the by-election of 1913.

Neither Mary nor I were able to go, we left this to the younger women, but we were always ready to support the cause. After In September of that year, Mary was asked to give an interview for the publication entitled the *Christian Commonwealth*. Before the interview, we discussed our many tramping experiences. Mary relished the chance to talk to the press about her experiences of the Tramp Wards. The reporter asked her why she embarked on the investigations. Mary explained that she had spoken to many destitute women about their experiences,

'I learned from the women's reports that the tramp ward was worse than useless; they left the wards without means to begin life afresh, and I found on investigation that the common lodging houses were in such a state of insanitation and offered so many temptations that a woman would inevitably lose her self-respect, if not her character, by entering them. I resolved to go and find out for myself by putting myself in their place.'

Mary said that she was shocked and utterly astonished by the conditions in the tramp wards and the common lodging houses. Of the tramp wards she declared,

'They exploit poor women. No lady would think of requiring of her charwoman on three good meals a day the work required of a tramp on bread and skilly with 1 ½ ozs of cheese at midday. Moreover, a woman's clothes become dirty through the menial work she is required to perform, and, though a bath is insisted upon, her old clothes are all she had to work in, and she goes out of the ward no better, but rather worse from the point of view of cleanliness, and the wearier and more discouraged, than when she went in.'
(Skilly is a sort of thin porridge, usually with a bit of meat in it.)

When asked about the common lodging houses she said,

'I could not believe that such conditions of dirt, vermin, overcrowding, and lack of sanitation would be tolerated by municipal

authorities. I saw at a glance the inevitableness of the degradation of a woman forced into such surroundings.'

In all the years I knew Mary, she never overlooked an opportunity to gain publicity for a worthy cause, or a chance to put forward her well thought out ideas. She felt strongly that every town should have at least one home in municipal control, so that it could be well regulated and free from the difficulties of having to rely on charity for its upkeep. To this end, she called for councils to provide overseen accommodation for women. As ever, her words were forceful and her ideas clear,

'I regard it as a communal duty to provide for women a substitute for common lodging-houses, so that the mixed common lodging-houses should be altogether suppressed. Couples are better in furnished rooms, where their children are also in less danger. The municipality must in time have these too under stricter supervision.'

She also stressed the ease with which women could turn to prostitution,

'I now understand that though there are not nearly as many women vagrants as men, or women in common lodging-houses, it is only because before they quite reach the state of the man who travels up and down the country living by beggary and theft they are forced to sell themselves for bread.'

Far more could be done, by providing well ventilated, women's lodging houses *'under the care of wise, motherly women'* that should be open to all women, even prostitutes.

Chapter 11 War is Declared

In February 1914, Mary reached her 60th birthday, with no sign of slowing down.   However, very soon events in Europe would overshadow our lives and provide another set of challenges.

When war was declared, many women in the cotton industry found themselves unemployed because the mills were unable to get raw materials from abroad. By September 1914, a month after the start of the war, well over 40% of women were out of work in Oldham. There was very little in the way of financial help from the government and soldiers' army pay did not arrive immediately. Help for the women and their children was urgently needed and a group of women including Sarah, Marjory and Mary, wasted no time in formulating a plan. The Oldham Committee for the Care of Women and Children was formed with the objective of setting up a workshop.   Premises, materials and staff were needed, so in October 1914, Mary wrote to Mr. Nadin of the Oldham Relief Committee outlining the plans. The town council provided a disused public house in the town centre, to serve as a clothes depot. It amazes me how quickly something can be done when there is a real will, and Mary had the will. Very soon, the scheme was in force at Bent House. The scheme ran from 9.00 am until 12.00 noon and from 2.00 pm until 4.00 pm on Monday, Tuesday, Thursday and Friday.   Women over 18 were paid five shillings for a 20-hour week and girls under 18 received four shillings. This worked well and we were soon able to find work for 20 women, 10 girls, a cutter and a supervisor. Mary was understandably proud of what we had done in such a short time, so she decided that the Palace should know about our success. She wrote a letter to Queen Mary's Lady in Waiting. The Queen, who knew of our work at Bent House, must have been impressed by our endeavours, because this led to the establishment of the Queen Mary workrooms throughout the country. Women made new clothes, blankets and uniforms for the forces. The Suffragette, Sylvia Pankhurst, daughter of Emmeline, was critical of the Queen Mary workrooms, also known as the Queen Mary's Work for Women Fund. She claimed that they usually paid below the going rate and often involved making new clothes out of old, but lacked any proper training. With such a high level of unemployment, the women had little choice, and certainly in the case of Oldham, Mary and the others running the scheme were making a real effort to reduce the level of poverty and keep the women purposefully occupied. This must have saved many women and their children from destitution at this very difficult time.

Around this period, Mary wrote a booklet entitled, *A Safe Place to Stay* to encourage women to use well-run hostels and lodging houses such as ours in Oldham. Instead of just producing a factual handbook, Mary used the idea of a short story featuring a conversation between two women about finding somewhere to stay. One of the women wants to visit her sister, but there is not enough room. The other woman recommends a lodging house.

'A lodging house? I've heard tell they are terrible rough places.'

Her advisor describes Ashton House, the Municipal lodging house in Manchester and says of Oldham's Bent House, 'They often bake their own bread.'

The hostels at Bent House and Hope House were usually full. At the beginning of 1916, Mary wrote a report of the work done during the previous year. She said that a *'steady stream of women and girls were given temporary shelter, some until they find their last home'*. Hawkers turned up on a regular basis and the police often sent girls in danger to us for their own safety. Mary was pleased that some women kept in touch by writing letters, and must have felt very gratified when one woman wrote saying that she wished that there were places like that everywhere and that, *'The ladies know what us poor women have to put up with.'*

Gradually, more work became available when the munitions plants started to employ women and Mary made it her business to visit the munitions hostels to make sure the conditions were satisfactory. Bent House was used as a centre for the payment of war pension and was a base for other organizations such as the Tipperary Club. This was a women's recreation club, which provided activities for the wives of service men on similar lines to the YMCA. The war occasioned another change for Mary. She was totally against conscription and started to question the whole validity of war. Consequently, she became a pacifist and member of the Religious Society of Friends (The Quakers) around 1916. Although she had been a Congregationalist all her life, she now embraced the Quaker belief and became an elder at the meeting house in Greaves Street, Oldham. She served on a number of committees such as the Vagrancy Committee and its various off-shoots, and as a representative for Lancashire and Cheshire, regularly attended meetings and conferences at The Friends' House in Euston Road, London.

Mary used her love of poetry to express her feelings about the futility of war. She explores the way in which England has been proud of the Empire, but she reminds readers that our mixed blood is the result of the many people who made this their home in the past. Her pacifism is reflected in this poem that ends by declaring that England cannot be truly free without peace.

> *'A war to end war,' brave men said,*
> *And flung their lives within the trench;*
> *They see their life-blood flowing red,*
> *They cared not for the reek and stench,*
> *So that Old England might be free,*
> *The land of truth and liberty.*
> *But these; these too are stalwart sons,*
> *And they see further; England Free?*
> *Yea! But 'a war to end war!' runs*
> *No patent right to liberty*
> *The WORLD must freedom claim, and be*
> *Set free from warfare's tyranny*

(From An Octave of Song
Published Easter 1917)

It was the start of a new era as Mary moved with Arthur, Lallie and their children, Barbara born in 1914 and Thomas born in 1917, from Bent Cottage to rooms in Bent House, a place that was to be her home for the rest of her life. All Mary's children were now settled and independent. Mary, the eldest was an unmarried classics mistress at Glasgow High School.

The Religious Society of Friends (Quakers) Meeting House in Greaves Street, Oldham

The Friends' Meeting House in Euston Road, London

Margaret, who also never married, was a district nurse in Somerset. Her youngest daughter, Mabel, who had given birth to a daughter, Edith in 1913, lived with her husband, a Justice of the Peace in Berkshire. This was, Mary reasoned, a good time to write a will.

She decided to leave everything to her unmarried daughter Margaret, *'with the understanding that she carries out my written and verbal instructions.'* I wonder what the instructions were and if they ever changed over the next 20 years? Despite her Congregational upbringing, Mary's hand written instruction was that she wanted to be cremated in keeping with her Quaker belief.

It was 11 years since we had first walked into the empty building, now we had both made our homes at Bent House. Many homeless women and girls had benefited from having somewhere safe to stay. Some had stayed only a night or two, but others had stayed longer and many returned. Before the end of 1917, there were some changes at Bent House. At a meeting on 14th December, it was decided that the Oldham Committee for the Care of Women and Children be renamed The Oldham Council of Social Welfare. The aim of the new council was, *'to promote Voluntary Endeavour and Social Service, and to provide a Bureau of Information on matters relating to public welfare'.* There were 43 representatives of various bodies, such as The Board of Guardians and the Beautiful Oldham Society. The first joint Honorary Secretaries were Clifford Atkins and Marjory Lees. Subcommittees such as; the Case Committee, the Juvenile Organization Committee, the Social Improvement Committee and the Education Committee were formed from the Executive Committee.

Regardless of the grim reality of the war, Mary remained optimistic and continued to encourage others to improve the environment of the town. Mary's love of, and commitment to, Oldham continued throughout her life. She always had the ability to see beyond the mills and appreciate the countryside. In March 1917, Mary gave a talk to a meeting of the Lancashire Authors' Association of which she was an active member. Speaking about *Beautiful Oldham* at Werneth Park, she expressed her love of the town and the surrounding countryside,

'Here stands our Town Hall – not much to look at, but centre of our civic hope and pride. Yonder towers our old church; monument of the life of the past; round it quiet rows of graves. Old Oldhamers, ye built well!
Here is the narrow street, once the old lane, through which passed your concentrated lives. Beyond stretched the moors; now the rows of

cottages, overshadowed by the great bulk of mills. But now we leave the street. We dodge round the newest mill, we pass the last cottage, and lo! A silent valley, save for the roar of innumerable wavelets of water. Down stone steps they run with roar and dash, and into the old original pool, and into the newer reservoir. Behind them is the dammed-up force of two reservoirs, of which they are merely the overflow! And here in the silent valley Nature again asserts herself. The moon faintly struggles through the cloud, waves lap, and lights gleam faintly. All is mystery and silence, save for the falling water. Here you may sit and dream. Here is peace. 'Beautiful Oldham!' which are you – the stream of human life, or the natural beauty of solitude, which encompasses you on every side?'

The passage which I believe describes Waterhead, an area close to Greenacres, was printed in the *Accrington Gazette*.

The end of the war came in 1918. Time for everyone to try to return to some form of normality. At last women over 30 were granted the vote. Mary wrote that her:

'Voice and pen were at the service of the cause, which she hardly expected to see victorious in her lifetime.'

Two years later the Oldham Women Citizens' Association was formed and not surprisingly, Mary, Sarah (by that time a Dame) and Marjory were actively involved.

Mary and her extended family were settled into the rooms at Bent House when tragedy struck. Her daughter-in-law, Lallie, contracted cancer and died in 1919 at the young age of 33. The death of the young mother must have caused a great deal of upset and upheaval to all the family. Arthur and his children, who were only five and two, continued to live with Mary until the time when he remarried.

Life went on, and in February 1924, Mary reached the age of 70. *The Oldham Chronicle* wrote a summary of her life and The Oldham Women Citizens' Association presented her with a beautifully bound book that honoured her achievements in Social Service. The album, bound in blue and gold, was in the form of a letter which started,

Dear Mrs. Higgs,

On the occasion of your 70th birthday you will have had many congratulations, and we also desire to tell you of our admiration and regard.

The letter goes on to detail her many achievements and says:

The tide of new ideas is rising. One by one, you are seeing your hopes made certainties and we, your fellow- workers, rejoice with you. You have done much for the town. You have grown to care. Few have met more personal in its relationships. The desire to create beauty has reigned in your heart. You have created hope by the human touch. Your sympathy has had imagination and insight. You have helped us to see your vision of the future. You have said, 'Grow old along with me. The best is yet to be.'

It was signed on behalf of the Society by Marjory Lees, President; Elizabeth Henderson, Honorary Treasurer; and Mary Claydon, Honorary Secretary. A copy of the address was printed in the *Oldham Chronicle* in May 1924. Mary, writing under the pseudonym of Mrs. Minerva, described the presentation with pride in her letter to *Young Oldhamer.* In turn, she praised the friendliness of the people of the town.

'It is one of the beauties of Oldham that it is so friendly! Privately, Mrs. Minerva thinks there isn't another place like it in the world, for just this simple friendliness. It travels from Mayor to street sweeper. It looks out of the houses, doors, it journeys in the trams, it gathers in innumerable meetings. If you meet an Oldhamer far away across the seas, or anywhere, it is quite enough that he or she is an Oldhamer, no other passport is needed into the heart's affections. This is a great asset.'

Despite reaching 70, Mary was still active in many areas of social reform. The level of unemployment in the post war years was very severe. Mary put a lot of her time and energy into looking for ways to alleviate some of the resulting distress and was instrumental in starting a paper-sorting enterprise for unemployed lads in Oldham. When her reports on vagrancy were republished in 1924 as *Down and Out*, it brought her into contact with the Society of Wayfarers' Benevolent Association, a group with whom she would work closely in the coming years. To show her continued concern and no doubt to gain publicity for the cause, she spent a night sleeping in the crypt of St. Martin's in London, with homeless men and women.

In the midst of what she referred to as an 'expansion of life' Mary suffered another personal loss. Her only son Arthur died of cancer in 1926, at the early age of 44, leaving two children, Barbara aged 12 and Thomas aged 9. Mary believed that the children should not be looked after by their stepmother, despite the fact that they had become very fond of her. Undoubtedly, it would have been difficult for Arthur's widow to financially support them. Barbara later told me that she sensed that her grandmother felt that her father had 'married below himself'. Therefore, it was decided that Thomas would stay with Mary. Having lost her only son, Mary told me that she felt some comfort in having her grandson living with her at Bent House until he was ready to go to boarding school. Barbara, by then a pupil at Hulme Grammar School for Girls, was sent to live with Mary's daughter, Margaret in Shepton Mallet, Somerset. Margaret and her sister Mary jointly owned a house named 'Greenaces' after the area in which they had been brought up, although Mary was away at school during term time. I did not know much about Margaret, only that she was single, had been a kindergarten teacher and later became a district nurse. However, I had seen Barbara grow up and could see how very upset she was about being sent away from the stepmother and brother that she loved. Unfortunately, Barbara did not get on well with her aunt, feeling that she was an intrusion in her aunt's single life.

No doubt Mary felt that the children would benefit from the arrangement in the long term, but it must have been quite a wrench for them to be separated from their stepmother and each other at that sad time.

Not long after this, Mary suffered a serious illness and spent four months in Shepton Mallet. Despite her ill health, Mary was still in touch with her fellow workers who took over her duties in Oldham. In her letter to me, she philosophically described the time as one of 'rest and reflection.'

Bent House continued to be a base for many clubs, meetings and activities. Some were long running such as the Oldham Branch of the Workers' Educational Association (WEA) and the Beautiful Oldham Society, which had been flourishing for about 25 years. The Oldham Christian Endeavour Comradeship had grown in connection with the C.E. Holiday Homes and their Executive Committee met at Bent House. Around this time, a young man who had been helped by Jennie Wareing asked Mary to write a biography of her life. The book entitled *Mother Wareing* was published about 1925 with a preface from Dr. Clark the founder of the Christian Endeavour Society. It is unusual to find biographies of working class women like Jennie. She had been a weaver in the Middleton area of Rochdale before becoming involved with the society. When Mary first came to Oldham, she had been influenced and inspired by the work of Jennie.

Mary wrote and published yearly reports on the social work and other activities centred in and around Bent House. In 1927, one improvement reported was the appointment of Lady Guardians to visit the Maternity Wards of the workhouse. Although pregnant women still went to Bent House, Mary considered that the best option was to send them to the Maternity Ward. It was almost impossible for a young woman to support a child alone. Most were given the support of their families, but those without help were now able to go to the new Salvation Army Rescue Home in Manchester. I continued to live and work at Bent House, but also visited the home run by the Salvation Army. I was in complete agreement with their aims and was later to become a member of the Army. We found that in addition to the needs of young women, there was also a grave need for accommodation for the elderly and middle-aged women who found they were, in Mary's words, 'squeezed out of homes by shortage of accommodation'. They did not want to go to the workhouse, so many stayed with us until they died. There was a constant flow of women who needed help. As soon as we had space, another woman filled it immediately.

In addition to the activities and meetings aimed at adults, such as the Adult School and the Mother's Meetings, were those designed to encourage the young of the town. The number of evening play centres had increased to three. The Young Oldham Society had been on rambles and the Junior Society members were taken to see the 'town's assets' such as the fire station, and gas works. The report of the following year, 1928, showed that, as some groups or societies ran their course, others took their place. For example the Poetry Society had 'died a natural death', but a reading circle had been set up. A Junior School had been created as a 'child' of the Adult School. Mary was pleased to report that a group of men who met at Bent House, the Oldham Unemployed Football Club, had created a football pitch out of waste town land. Each Monday, men who wanted allotments, also met at Bent House. In fact, Mary, with her usual humour and lack of pomposity, made the pun that Bent House was, 'bent to every useful purpose'.

Eventually, in 1928, the Representation of People Act granted all women over twenty one the right to vote, and Mary and I had lived to see it! Mary felt that other aspects of the law needed changing. She was concerned about homeless boys becoming criminals and said to me, 'These boys should not be put into prison.'
'What crimes are they accused of?' I asked.
'They are brought before the magistrates for the offence of vagrancy. Reform is needed.   I've written to the Guardians of all the workhouses and to all the Justices of the Peace, setting out our suggestions.'
'Whose suggestions?'
'The Vagrancy Reform Society of the Quakers. We want to set up our own home for these boys, a sort of probation colony. We believe that the help given to the boys will keep them out of trouble and get them into work.'
'That sounds like a very good idea, but where will the money come from?'
'I've been busy writing letters to try to raise funds. The Wayfarers have promised to give money from their benefit fund, and we're hopeful of getting subscriptions and donations. We're also looking to get money from the local authority.'
On 1st December 1929 Moore Place, (an old manor house set in fifteen and half acres in Stanford le Hope, Essex) was acquired on

lease, but funds were needed for repair. The following April I was invited to go with Mary to visit the home. We arrived on the train from London where we had been staying. The sun shone as we walked from the station. The house, Mary told me, was about three quarters of a mile outside Stanford le Hope on Southend Road. It was surrounded by trees whose leaves of various shades of green were starting to open, as the weather grew warmer. As we walked down the driveway, Mary told me that there was a mature orchard behind the house, which would provide fruit later in the year. We passed a group of lads sawing logs.

'Hello, Mother Mary,' called a lad who looked about 15.

'Good morning, Bill, and who is this working with you?'

'This is Tom, Mother Mary, he cum here last week.'

'Good morning, Tom.' The taller lad looked up and smiled rather shyly at Mary.

'You look busy, so we'll let you get on.'

I could see the house through the trees, as we got close. It looked very grand. It had an impressive front porch with two wide, Greek style stone pillars holding up a stone roof. The tops of the pillars had carved coils at the side, similar to those at the front of Oldham Town hall. The wide wooden door had been painted dark green and the black metal bell and its hangings looked newly painted.

In front of the house was a wooden bench. We walked around to the back of the house to a large greenhouse where a couple of lads were watering plants.

'Hello Mother Mary.'

'Hello lads, what's growing here?'

'There are tomatoes what we planted in January, and these are radishes.'

Mary pointed to other seedlings, 'What are these?'

'Broad beans and them's cabbage.'

'Good work, lads!'

'Thank you Mother Mary,' said the boys.

Around the door of the house, four speckled hens clustered in the hope of some titbits. The lads shooed them away and closed the door after us.

'Are there other animals?' I asked.

'Yes, let's go and see the goats.'

An old wooden barn stood to our left. Some lads were working on repairs to the building.

'We will use the barn to house older men,' said Mary.

'Good morning Mrs. Higgs.'

A man of about 49 was giving advice and general supervision. Mary introduced us. I found that Mr. Hepworth lived at the hostel with his wife and daughter. Mrs. Hepworth acted as a matron and was well liked by the boys. Mary wanted to foster a family atmosphere so the boys were encouraged to call her Mother Alice. Passing other poultry on the way I was aware of the smell of animals. Two goats were in a small enclosure, but some boys were working to extend it. On the way back to the house we passed lads mulching vegetable plots and we could hear the sound of other lads chopping wood for the fires. All those we passed looked content and some were singing as they worked.

'We should be able to grow most of our vegetables,' said Mary,

'And we have eggs from chickens and milk from goats.'

Most of the boys were in the 14 to 18 age group and all were under 25.

'All the lads have been living rough on the road. Many are motherless or fatherless, or both. For instance, the lad Bill we met sawing wood, he's only 15 and doesn't know his father. His mother is a hawker, but she makes very little money. They both ended up in the workhouse. Bill left as soon as he could to try to find work, but had been sleeping rough and was brought before the magistrates for vagrancy. He was sent here and proved to be a hardworking lad. It is hoped that he will learn the skills to find work on a farm. Another lad is 16 and has lost both his parents. He had started an apprenticeship in Southend, but when his parents died, he had to leave to try to support his younger siblings. He managed to get a job looking after horses at the stables of a large house, but the owners decided that they could no longer afford the horses and had to let him go. Since then he's managed to get seasonal work, but all winter he's been tramping and sleeping outside. He's a bright lad and eager to learn new skills. He would like to learn carpentry.'

'Do all the boys receive some training?'

'Yes and a home until they can be placed in permanent jobs. It's time for lunch.'

We went inside the house. The front door led onto a large hallway with a very high ceiling. Doors to the left and right led from the hall and a staircase ran up the middle. The smell of freshly baked bread and coffee wafted along the corridor.

In the spacious kitchen, we meet Mrs. Hepworth, known to the lads as Mother Alice. After an introduction and a warm welcome, we were directed to a large scrubbed table. A group of lads came in and sat on the benches with us.

We were given large bowls of steaming vegetable and barley soup with fresh crusty bread and some goat's cheese. There was salt, pepper and butter on the table and a large jug of water and glasses. Alice asked Mary to say grace. The boys ate hungrily, dipping chunks of bread into the hearty soup. It was gratifying to watch them, and even though I was not a mother, I could feel a rush of maternal concern for these unfortunate lads.

'This beats gruel any day,' I said enjoying the tasty soup. I had never had goat's cheese before, and I found the flavour a little strange, but not unpleasant. When the bowls were empty, Alice's daughter Evelyn brought a large egg custard and a pot of freshly brewed coffee. As we were finishing, we could hear the next group coming in from washing their hands at the back of the house. We helped Alice and Evelyn clear the table ready for the next sitting. Our group of lads thanked them and went out to continue with their chores. Mary wanted to show me around the rest of the smallholding. It covered 15 acres, so there was a great deal of scope to expand, and it was intended to be almost self-sufficient by the end of the year.

During the afternoon, a boy about 14 came to the house. He had been sent by the police when a farmer had found him sleeping in his barn. His name was Gilbert and he told a sorry tale. His father, a man who became violent after drink, had left his mother over a year ago. Gilbert had left school and gone on the road with his mother who tried to earn money by charring. She had become ill and had been obliged to go to the workhouse for help. Gilbert had tried to find work, but he had neither skills nor experience. He had been sleeping outside before he found a barn to sleep in. He said that he was eager to learn a skill to provide for himself and mother.

'Having slept rough, there is a high chance of personal vermin,' said Mary.

'He will have a bath and a change of clothes and sleep in our special department before it's decided if he will be admitted.'

'How is it decided if he will be admitted?'

'He will be interviewed to see if he is capable and willing to undertake training and advice. If he is accepted he will be clothed, fed, and given some means of livelihood.'

After our evening meal, there was what Mary called 'family prayers.' She told me that she wanted to create a family atmosphere for the boys, and that she liked to be known as 'Mother Mary.'

This was my only visit to Moore Place but Mary, who made the journey every month, kept me informed of the progress. As secretary, she produced reports about the activities, with a balance sheet, and took the opportunity to encourage donations of money and clothing, especially boots.

Mary was proud to tell me that she personally visited every hostel in England that had been set up to receive homeless boys.

A pamphlet was produced to help raise funds

Chapter 12 An Invitation to the Palace

The depression of the 1930s caused mass unemployment and many families found their main breadwinner out of work for long periods. In January 1930 Mary was a convener on the Vagrancy Committee of the Quakers. That month she wrote a letter to the *Manchester Guardian* entitled *Test Work – Why Not Training for Labour.* In September of that year, after much campaigning, the Ministry of Health set up a Committee of Inquiry into Casual Ward Reform. Representatives from the Home Office and the Ministry of Labour were present and Mary was asked to give evidence. She spoke for four hours, putting before them a scheme for Vagrancy Reform, which the Quaker's Vagrancy Committee had previously approved.

In her late seventies, Mary was still practically involved in many schemes, but in 1932, she became ill and had to miss several meetings. She soon recovered and managed to attend the Annual Meeting of the Wayfarers' Benevolent Association at Harrogate.

Her commitment to Oldham continued. She gave a talk about the Oldham Casual Ward at Oldham Men's Institute during 1932, and she was instrumental in setting up a school for unemployed boys. She was happy to report that the Fellowship Hostels in the town centre 'are proving the means of bring the men back to work.'

A year later, in 1933, Mary was involved in starting a Fellowship Service Club as a place for the unemployed men of Oldham to meet. This was inspired by the clubs Mary had visited in the Rhondda Valley. They had been funded by the Lord Mayor of London's scheme to help relieve the poverty in the Welsh coalfields. In Oldham, the scheme was organised by the Service Committee of the Oldham Quakers and set up at a house at 29 New Ratcliffe Street in the town centre, not far from West Street. The following year, the Committee acquired another two houses in the town centre. Part of the house in Beechy Street was occupied by the Secretary and his family and the rest was rented out to others in need of accommodation. Not long after, a large house in Eden Street was acquired. It was furnished for 16 men, and a warden and his family moved in ready to help those in need. The setting up of these hostels went some way to alleviating a very urgent problem.

Mary had made many friends during her long and active lifetime. At Christmas 1933, she wrote an open letter describing life as music, the rhythm of work and rest. She also wrote about being away from friends but believed that prayer could join them, ending the letter,

'With this prayer for you, I am, yours in His love and service, Mary Higgs (and to not a few 'Mother Mary').

In 1934, a large party was given at the Friends' Meeting House in London to celebrate Mary's 80th birthday. A young man from Moore Place Hostel was invited to light the candles on her cake. Mary gave a speech appealing for 'more humane consideration and better provision of those on the road'.

Throughout that year Mary was still active, writing letters and articles, attending meetings and overseeing work in Oldham and Essex. For example, she wrote three letters to the *Times* on the subject of the Casual Ward, published on 26th June, 6th July and 9th July 1934. Over her many years in Oldham, she had built up a good relationship with the editors of the local newspapers to which she contributed regular letters, and she also wrote articles for *Northern Voice*, the weekly paper of the Lancashire division of the Independent Labour Party. Mary was 82 in 1936, but continued a rate of work which would have tired a much younger person. Much of her time was taken as a representative of Quaker committees. In addition to being the representative for Lancashire and Cheshire of the Meeting for Sufferings and the Service Council, she was asked to become a trustee of Moore Place. In May, she spoke at Hyde Park and later gave a talk on vagrancy at the Bristol and Somerset Quarterly Meeting.
Back in Oldham, Mary and her co-workers wanted to help men who would otherwise have to go into institutions. So the women who were staying in Hope House were moved to Bent House and Bent Cottage, leaving Hope House available for homeless men.

Mary Higgs

Mary encouraged the people of Oldham to contribute to the scheme and also received donations from 'Old Oldhamers' (those who had left the town and were living elsewhere in the country or abroad). Her quest to effect change continued. She wrote a paper on the Collective Provision for the Permanently Poor and the *Oldham Chronicle* published her article about Fellowship Hostels under the title *How Fellowship Hostels Help Those in Distress*. She describes how clubs had been set up and gave examples of the dire straits in which some single unemployed men found themselves. For instance, an unemployed cotton worker who received 17 shillings and he had to pay 10 shillings out of that for bed, light and washing, leaving just seven shillings a week for food and all other expenses. The work was having an influence in other parts of the country. Mary reported that they had received enquires from a number of places including London and it would not be long before she would receive further recognition for her work. She wrote,

'Those well acquainted with the homeless poor problem are becoming convinced that small family hostels are better than large barrack-like ones, both for boys and men.'

Bent House, West Street

This was taken at a later date than the previous photograph. The building was demolished during the 1960s.

They were leading the way, and with the change in the benefits from Poor Law to National Assistance, Mary believed that this was a great opportunity to find accommodation for the unemployed.

Mary's family and friends were spread around the country. After spending Christmas of 1936 with her family at the home of daughter Margaret in Shepton Mallet, she wrote to me and other friends,

'It is wonderful how many things God puts into life if you try daily and hourly to follow His will.'

The New Year brought news that she was to be awarded the Officer's medal, Civil Division of the Most Excellent Order of the British Empire (OBE). This followed a recommendation from the Mayor of Oldham Alderman R.W Bainbridge J.P. The 2nd February was her 83rd birthday and she was happy to spend it at Moore Place Hostel among friends. To mark the occasion photographs were taken and she was interviewed by reporters. She wrote to me about the celebration and the forthcoming honour. With her usual humour she said that she would have to 'dress up' for the occasion, but would just as soon wear the clothes she wore when we went 'on the tramp'.

On 25th February 1937 Mary Ann Higgs arrived at the Buckingham Palace dressed in her best clothes.
King George V1 presented her with the Order of the British Empire, *'For Public Services to Oldham'.*
After the ceremony, she felt tired and decided to go to her daughter Mary's home in Greenwich. She had to cancel other engagements in order to rest and was visited by friends. Nevertheless, she still found the strength to write her *Young Oldhamer* letter and sent the medal 'for the children to see at the spring meeting of the Beautiful Oldham Society.'
She also managed to write to me and other friends about the occasion. She told me that she had been pleased to speak to the King about his interest in Lancashire Boys' Clubs. Sadly, I never saw Mary again. She never regained enough strength to return to Oldham. Only 22 days after receiving the OBE from the hands of the King, she passed away at the home of her daughter Mary. It was heartening that she

had received the well-overdue official recognition while she was still alive. She died on 19th March, I would say aptly, on the first day of the spring exhibition of the Beautiful Oldham Society, where she would be sadly missed.

The reporter for *Oldham Chronicle* showed his shock at her death when he reported the following day:

...but as no intimation of a breakdown in her health had been received in the town, the news last night came with distressing suddenness.

The medal, certificate and photograph of Mary Higgs as displayed in Oldham

In addition to the obituary in the Oldham paper, the *Manchester Guardian*, *The Times*, the *Daily Herald,* and the *Daily Dispatch* reported her passing.

The Times (20th March) carried the notice:

Higgs – *on March 19th 1937 at 4 McCartney House, Greenwich, MARY HIGGS, M.A., O.B.E. of Bent House, Oldham, in her 84th* *year. Cremation, Golders Green 2.30 p.m. Tuesday. Date of funeral at Oldham to be announced later.*

Mary's name and work were internationally recognized. The *New York Times* considered her to be of significant importance to carry an obituary on Sunday 21st March, which began:

MRS. MARY HIGGS; British Woman Honored for her Social Service Work
Mrs. Mary Higgs of Oldham, Lancashire, whose life was devoted to social work, particularly on behalf of friendless tramps, died at the age of 83. In the last honors list she was received into the Order of the British Empire.

The news of her death was even reported as far away as Australia. *The Examiner*, published in Launceston Tasmania, reported on Monday 22nd March 1937:

Social Worker's Death
London March 20th
The death occurred yesterday of Mrs. Mary Higgs of Oldham, Lancashire, aged 83, whose life was devoted to social work, particularly on behalf of friendless tramps. In the last Honours list she was awarded the OBE.

On the same day (22nd March) the following report appeared in *The Times:*

The entourage left her daughter's home at McCartney House, Chesterfield Walk, Greenwich on 23 March for a cremation at Golders Green. Her ashes were taken to Oldham to be interred in the cemetery of Greenacres Congregational Church.

Mary was brought up as a Congregationalist, and although she had become a Quaker, her ashes were to be buried with the bodies of her husband, son and daughter-in-law. A Memorial Service was held at Greenacres Congregation Chapel on Saturday 3rd April 1937. In addition to her relatives and many friends, including Marjory Lees,

representatives from the many associations with which Mary had been connected crowded into the chapel to pay their respects, for example:
The Beautiful Oldham Society,
The Council of Social Welfare,
The League of Service,
Oldham Women Citizen's Association,
Oldham Women Unionist Association,
The National Women's Total Abstinence,
The National Union of Women Teachers,
The Wayfarers' Benevolent Association,
The Lancashire Mental Hospital Board,
The Workers' Educational Association,
Grosvenor Hall,
Oldham Town Mission,
The Assistant Director of Education,
The Chief Constable,
The Medical Health Officer

The Rev J. Arnold Quail of Greenacres Congregational Chapel spoke about her life,

'She had done much good by translating her dreams into effect. She had dreams of beauty that she dreamed as soon as she came to Oldham, the dream of guarding the lives of the poorest of her sisters. She was enthusiastic about her work and was able to encourage others to help her.'

He ended by saying that he hoped that others would carry on 'translating' now she had gone.

It seems ironic that Mary should die three weeks after gaining official recognition from the Palace. It was as though she had hung on to life for that day, and then, tired out with all her good work, let go. At last she could, as she would say, 'go home'.

159

The grave of Rev Thomas Higgs, Alice Higgs, Arthur Higgs and Mary Higgs is marked by horizontal stones. The church stands in the background.

Postscript

Mary's last work, entitled Christ's Miracles of Healing, contained extracts from William Stead's diary, The Way of the Joyous Life. Her friend, J.L. Paton, who published the book after her death in 1937, described it as, 'A Voice From Beyond.'
The reviewer for the *Chronicle*, H.G.G. wrote,

'The essay is an interesting discussion, in the form of conversations, with a commentary on the healing miracles of Jesus, and lovers of the works of Mrs. Higgs, as well as those who know and sympathise with the objects she upheld, will be glad of the opportunity of reading another work from her pen.'

In memory of Mary Higgs a laburnum tree was planted in Werneth Park in 1938 by member of the Beautiful Oldham Society. A bronze covered plaster bust was made. This was in the possession of Oldham Museum, but is now missing.

The Mary Higgs Memorial Fund was set up to support Moore Place. By October 1938, it was seen that the £650 raised was not sufficient to purchase the property. Therefore, it was decided to try to raise further funds. The following February the amount had risen to £700.

It has been decided to invest the £700 collected, and to use the interest to pay part of the rent of the Moore Place Hostel for young Way Farers.
A trust investment has been secured, yielding £28 per annum; to this sum, the Vagrancy Reform Society will, for the present, add £4 per annum. It will thus be possible to materially help the Hostel, while still retaining the power to realise the capital if it is desired, at a later stage, to purchase premises.

In the 1950s her eldest daughter wrote a biography, but only a limited number were produced for private circulation. Copies of many of Mary's books and her medal were given to the museum/library in Oldham.

Although the idea of a "Beautiful Oldham" was ridiculed by many, the Society undoubtedly achieved some measure of success. Many Oldhamers will remember the annual shows and competitions with affection. Schools encouraged children to plant spring bulbs which they sold at reasonable prices, and to draw and colour pictures of plants to enter the yearly competitions. The prizes were presented at Werneth Park and children received badges and certificates. In his memoir, *If I Don't Write it Nobody Else Will*, Eric Sykes recalls the time when his picture of spring flowers won him a prize.

The Beautiful Oldham Society introduced countless children who lived in houses without gardens, to the pleasure of planting bulbs and waiting for them to grow and to flower into a thing of beauty. The last spring flower show was held on 9th and 10th May 1990 at Werneth park music room.

In more recent years Higgs Close, a small development of seven semi detached houses was built in 1995. This is very close to Greenacres Church, so could also be named after Rev Higgs. In 2010 Mary's memory was kept alive when the Pupil Support Unit decided to use her maiden name when it changed its name to Kingsland School.

Mary was not a wealthy woman and left just over £200, possibly from the sale of the cottage near Hebden Bridge which was given to her by a friend. Her legacy was her inspiration and the influence she had on the many men, women and children whose lives she touched.

163

In His Majesty's High Court of Justice.
The Principal Probate Registry.

BE IT KNOWN that *Mary Ann Higgs*

of Bent House Oldham in the County of Lancaster widow

died on the *19th* day of *March* 193*7*

at 4 Macartney Home Chesterfield Walk Greenwich London S.E.10

AND BE IT FURTHER KNOWN that at the date hereunder written the last Will and Testament

(a copy whereof is hereunto annexed) of the said deceased was proved and registered in the Principal Probate Registry of His Majesty's High Court of Justice and that Administration of all the Estate which by law devolves to and vests in the personal representative of the said deceased was granted by the aforesaid Court to

Margaret Dorothy Higgs of Greenacres Shepton Mallet in the County of Somerset spinster daughter of deceased the sole executrix named in the said Will

And it is hereby certified that on Affidavit for Inland Revenue has been delivered wherein it is shown that the gross value of the said Estate in Great Britain (exclusive of what the said deceased may have been possessed of or entitled to as a Trustee and not beneficially) amounts to £ *221 15 1* and that the said Affidavit bears a stamp of £ *1 10 0*

Dated the *31st* day of *May* 193*7*

Registrar.

Probate Certificate

164

Literature by Mary Higgs

Approximate Dates

1904 The Twentieth Century New Testament
(Originally published in three parts between 1898 and 1901)
1905 How to Deal with the Unemployed
Five Days and Five Nights as a Tramp
The Master – The Wisdom of a Disciple
A Night in a Salvation Army Shelter
The Tramp Ward
Christ and His Miracle
The Bible – the Survival of the Fittest
1906 Essay on Vagrancy
Glimpses into the Abyss
Three Nights in Women's Lodging Houses
1910 Evolution of the Child Mind
The New Creation
Where Shall She Live?
Where Shall He Live?
History of the Beautiful Oldham Society
1912 How to Start a Woman's Lodging House
1914 A Safe Clean Place to Live
Where Shall She Live? – The Answer
My Brother the Tramp
1915 The Housing of the Woman Worker
An Octave of Song
1924 Mother Wareing
1928 Casuals and Their Casual Treatment
1929 The Collective Provision for
the Permanently Poor
1936 How Fellowship Hostels Help Those in Distress
1937 Christ's Miracles of Healing

Chronology of events

1854 Mary Ann Kingsland born on 2nd February
1855 William Kingsland (brother) born
1856 John Paddon (brother) born
1862 Family moved to Bradford
1869 Women's College at Hitchin founded
1871 Mary entered the Women's College
1873 Girton College opened
1874 Gained Natural Science Tripos
        Became assistant lecturer at Girton
1876 Began teaching in Bradford
1876 Rev William Kingsland (father) died aged 49
        Became engaged to Thomas Kilpin Higgs
1878 Thomas Higgs became minister at Hanley
1879 Married Rev Higgs
1880 Mary Kingsland Higgs (daughter) born - Stoke
1882 Arthur Hilton Higgs (son) born - Stoke
1888 Margaret Dorothy Higgs (daughter) born – Stoke
1890 Mabel Paddon Higgs (daughter) born Manchester
1891 Moved to Greenacres, Oldham
1892 Lock-out of Cotton Operatives in Oldham
1897 Oldham Branch of National Council of Women
1898 Ebenezer Howard's first book Tomorrow – a
        Peaceful Path to Real Reform published
1899 William T. Stead, spoke at Oldham Town Hall
1901 Queen Victoria died. Edward VII acceded.
1902 Beautiful Oldham Society founded
        Howard's Garden Cities of Tomorrow published
1903 First tramp experience
1906 Bent House acquired
1907 Rev Thomas Higgs (husband) died May aged 56
1907 Sarah Lees, became an Oldham Councillor
1908 National Association for Women's Lodging-Homes founded
1909 Lock-out of Cotton Operatives in Oldham
        Healey Street Mission Club opened in Oldham
1910 Attended a conference of the National Council of Women in
        Toronto.

1910 Sarah Lees became Mayor of Oldham
Oldham Women's Suffrage Society founded
Ashton House opened in Manchester

1911 Edward VII died. George V succeeded to the throne.

1912 Arthur (son) married Alice Dunkerley
Mabel (daughter) married Herbert Shawcross
William T. Stead went down with the Titanic

1913 King George V and Queen Mary visited Oldham

1914 **WW1 began**
Barbara Mary Higgs (granddaughter) born

1917 Thomas Peter Kingsland Higgs (grandson) born
Sarah Lees became a Dame

**1918 Women over 30 given vote in General
Election**

1919 Alice Higgs (daughter in law) died aged 33
Oldham Women Citizen's Association
Formed

1926 Arthur Hilton Higgs died in November
Aged 44

1928 Women over 21 granted the vote

1936 King George V died. Edward VIII
Abdicated, King George V1 acceded in
December

**1937 Mary Awarded OBE on 25th February
Mary Died on 19th March aged 83**

The Family of Mary Ann Higgs (nee Kingsland)

William Kingsland, Mary's father, was born in Hythe, Kent c1827. He studied theology at Western College Plymouth. In 1853 he married Caroline Paddon in Truro. The couple moved to Devises, Wiltshire where he was a Congregational Minister. The family – by then they had three children – moved to Bradford in 1862, when William became minister at College Chapel. He died in Bradford 1876, aged 49.

Caroline Eliza Paddon, Mary's mother, was born in Cornwall c1819. Her father was a Borough Magistrate and a Timber Merchant. She was 34 when she married William Kingsland. After the death of her husband, Caroline moved to Bristol. She later lived in Devon and then to Gower, South Wales. She died in 1911 in Axbridge, Somerset, aged 93.

William Kingsland, Mary's brother, was born in Devizes, Wiltshire in 1855. He became an Electrical Engineer and was a member of the Institute of Engineering and Technology. He married Phoebe Edmonstone. In 1901 the couple were living in Leamington Spa, Warwickshire. William became lecturer in astronomy and a prolific writer. He wrote such works as: Metaphysics and Theosophy and Rational Mysticism. When he died in Feb 1936, he was resident at 'Claremont', The Strand, Ryde, Isle of Wight and left over £2000 (some to his brother John). He had lived on the Island for many years and was a founding member of the Theosophical Society (Reported in Isle of Wight County Press, Ryde, IOW). His last book Gnosis or Ancient Wisdom in the Christian Scriptures or the Wisdom in a Mystery was published after his death in 1937.

John Paddon Kingsland, Mary's brother, was born in Devizes, Wiltshire in 1856. In 1878 he became a theology student at Lancashire Independent College. He married Helen Priscilla Perkins in Baron on Irwell, Lancashire in 1887. He held ministries in Macclesfield and Manchester before returning to Devizes, the place of his birth, from 1909 to 1917. He then moved to Victoria, St. Helier, and Jersey, where he remained until 1920. He became a Senior

Alumnus of the Lancashire Independent College. He died on 5th June 1945 in Felixstowe, aged 89.

Thomas Kilpin Higgs, Mary's husband, was born 1851 in Ipswich, Suffolk. He studied engineering at Manchester Victoria University and then theology at Lancashire Independent College. His first ministry was at the Tabernacle at Hanley, Stoke on Trent. He then moved to Withington Manchester, and finally to Greenacres Congregational Church Oldham. He died on 25 May 1907 in Oldham, aged 56.

Mary Kingsland Higgs, Mary's daughter, was born in 1880 in Hanley, Stoke. She won a scholarship to Manchester Girls' Grammar School. She then attended Westfield Ladies' College at Hampstead and St. Mary's Gate College. Her first teaching post was classical mistress at Kensington High School (1906-1912). She also taught at The Ladies' College Cheltenham (1912-1915), and Glasgow High School for Girls (1915-1919). In 1919 she became headmistress of Roan School for Girls Greenwich, South East London. She never married and died in 1964 in Bath, aged 84.

Arthur Hilton Higgs, Mary's son, was born in Hanley, Stoke on Trent in 1882. He became an Electrical Engineer with Ferranti in Oldham. He married Alice (Lallie) Dunkerley in 1912 in Oldham. Alice died in 1919 aged 33. In February of 1923 Arthur, of Ferranti Ltd. was named as the inventor of protective electrical switchgear, when patents were applied for. He married Phoebe Lewthwaite of Oldham in Nottingham in 1926. The couple lived in Dobcross, Saddleworth. Sadly Arthur contracted cancer and died soon after their marriage - November 1926 - at 31 York Place Chorlton in Medlock, Manchester, aged 42.

Margaret Dorothy Higgs, Mary's daughter, was born in 1888 in Hanley, Stoke. She attended Hulme Grammar School in Oldham. She worked as a kindergarten teacher and later became a district nurse. She lived at Green Acres, Shepton Mallet, Somerset, a house understood to be owned jointly with her sister Mary. Margaret was the executor of her mother's will and was still resident at Green Acres in 1937. She did not marry and died in 1979 in Mendip, Somerset, aged 91.

Mabel Paddon Higgs, Mary's daughter, was born in 1890 in Withington, Manchester. She also attended Hulme Grammar School in Oldham. She then became a student at Art College. She had a Quaker marriage to Herbert Tuer Shawcross in 1912 at Ulverston in the Lake District. In 1913 she gave birth to Edith. She died in 1942 in Wallingford aged 52.
Her husband was born in 1870, son of William Tuer Shawcross and Elizabeth Eckersley. He was educated at Giggleswick Grammar. He was a fruit farmer and held the office of Justice of the Peace for Berkshire from April 1914. At his death in 1961 he was living at Boar's Hill, Oxford, and Berkshire. His estate was worth over £45,000.

Edith Paddon Shawcross, Mary's granddaughter, was born 25 March 1913 to Mabel and Herbert Shawcross in Abington on the Buckinghamshire/Oxfordshire border. She graduated from St. Hilda's College, Oxford in 1935 with a Bachelor of Arts. She married Edward N Hall, an American, in 1943 and immigrated to the USA after the war.
The couple had three children. Edith died in 2009 in California, aged 96.
Her husband was born 4 Aug 1914 and became a Colonel in the US Air force. He died in 2006 aged 92.

Barbara Mary Higgs, Mary's granddaughter, was born in 1914 to Arthur and Alice in Oldham. She attended college and became a teacher of physical education. During WW2 she worked as a nurse in war-torn London. After the war she married Daniel Bergman in Taunton in 1945. The couple immigrated to the USA a year later. They had three sons. She died September 2009 in Virginia, aged 95.

Thomas Peter Kingsland Higgs, Mary's grandson, was born in 1917 to Arthur and Alice in Oldham. He attended the Royal Masonic School then Merton College, Cambridge. There he joined the University Air Squadron and took a direct-entry permanent commission with 111 squadron stationed at Croydon. On 9 August he was promoted from Pilot Officer to Flying Officer (service no. 36165). in 1940 he became the first casualty of the RAF in the Battle of Britain. He was apparently attacked by Oberlautenant Oesau of 111/JG51 over the English Channel off the coast of Folkestone. He then collided with a Do17 and lost a wing at 6,000 feet. He bailed out and his plane crashed. Despite rescue attempts, he drowned on 10th July 1940, aged 23. His body washed up at Noordwijk in Holland on 15 August. Thomas, known to his family as Peter, is buried in Noordwijk General Cemetery, Netherlands.

Thomas Peter Kingsland Higgs

Sources

Mary Higgs of Oldham by Mary Kingsland Higgs (printed for private circulation) 1954
Oldham Brave Oldham by Brian R Law (Oldham Council) 1999
A History of Oldham by Hartley Bateson (Oldham Council) 1949. Reprinted (The Amethyst Press) 1985
Greenacres Congregational Church by John Wibberley (Hirst, Kidd and Rennie Ltd) 1984

The British Library - Parliamentary papers
Oldham Chronicle Library - Photographs, letters, articles and obituary
Oldham Local Studies Library and Archives - Photographs, books, articles, maps, newspaper cuttings, letters and notes
Oldham Museum - Photographs of artefacts
Girton College Archives - Photographs of students and college, prospectus, letters by Emily Davies. Articles, song, poems etc by Mary Higgs (nee Kingsland). Details of Memorial fund set up after her death (Moore Place Hostel)
Bradford Local Studies Library - Photographs, maps, reports about Bradford Girls' Grammar School and the Salt Schools
Bradford Girls' Grammar School Archives - Yearly report books about Bradford Girls' Grammar School
The Religious Society of Friends (Quakers) Archives –London. Minutes, letters, reports etc.
The Probate Office - Will and probate
Times Newspaper - Archives Online-Letters, notices and obituary
New York Times Online - Obituary

Information about Mary Kingsland Higgs - (Mary's eldest daughter) **Manchester Girls' Grammar School archives** - Photos, year reports **Society of Genealogists** - Teachers' Registration **Greenwich Cultural and Community Service** - information and photograph from book The *History of the Roan School* by JW Kirby (Blackhealth Press) 1929

Further reading

People of the Abyss by Jack London (Macmillan) 1903
Fighters for the Poor – Martha Loane, Olive Malvery (Mackirdy) and Mary Higgs by Susan Cohen and Clive Fleay - an article in History Today, Jan 2000
Slumming by Seth Koven (Princetown University Press) 2001

Online Source - www.workhouses.or.uk by Peter Higginbotham

By the same publisher

Shadows – An Anthology of Short Stories. 2010

About the Author

Carol Mitchell Talbot was born and brought up in Oldham. She has two grown up sons and four grandchildren and lives in Saddleworth with her husband Nigel.

She taught in primary and adult education in the town and followed her interest in history by gaining an MA in the History of the Manchester Region at Manchester Metropolitan University.

Carol is a member of Manchester and Lancashire Family History Society, Lancashire Authors' Association, Lancashire and Cheshire Antiquarian Society, the Oldham branch of U3, Oldham Writing Café and Oldham Coliseum Full Circle. She enjoys visiting other countries. But most of all she loves to spend time with her family and friends.

You can order further copies of this book direct from the author via the website: www.caroltalbot.co.uk. Please state if you would like the author to sign it. You can use *PayPal*

Alternatively, send a copy of the coupon below to:

OWC Publishing
59 Heywood Ave
Oldham
OL4 4AZ

Please send me ___ copes of The Amazing Mary Higgs

I enclose a UK bank cheque payable to C Talbot for £_____ for __ copies @ £ 6.99 a copy + £2.50 per book post and packing (UK)

Please contact the author at info@caroltalbot.co.uk if ordering multiple copies or if outside the UK

NAME;
ADDRESS:
POSTCODE:
Email address or phone number:

Please allow 7 days for delivery from clearing of cheque. Do not send cash. Offer subject to availability. We do not share our customer's details.